THE LAST OF THE
LIGHTNINGS

Three Lightnings in formation. Led by the all-silver XP693, two former Binbrook aircraft make a farewell flypast over Warton in late December 1992. Nearest the camera is XR773 which had once been 'BR' on 11 Squadron. It had been stored at Boscombe Down before joining the remaining aircraft at Warton. Despite sitting for over a year on the ground the aircraft flew perfectly on its first flight, all systems working correctly, including the radar.

At the rear is XS904, an aircraft that spent all its life based in the UK, predominantly with 11 Squadron. This veteran Lightning completed over 4,000 flights and clocked up 4,161 flying hours. It holds the distinction of performing the last ever Lightning sortie when it was delivered to the Lightning Preservation Group on 21 January 1993.

As part of our ongoing market research, we are always pleased to receive comments about our books, suggestions for new titles, or requests for catalogues. Please write to: The Editorial Director, Patrick Stephens Limited, Sparkford, Nr Yeovil, Somerset BA22 7JJ

THE LAST OF THE
LIGHTNINGS

Ian Black

New Edition

SUTTON PUBLISHING

This book was first published in 1996 by Patrick Stephens Limited,
an imprint of Haynes Publishing

This new revised edition first published in 2002 by
Sutton Publishing Limited · Phoenix Mill
Thrupp · Stroud · Gloucestershire · GL5 2BU

British Library Cataloguing in Publication Data
A catalogue record for this book is available from the British Library

ISBN 0 7509 3073 X

All photography is by Ian Black, unless otherwise stated.

Printed and bound in Great Britain by
J.H. Haynes & Co. Ltd, Sparkford.

Contents

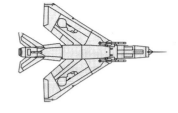

Acknowledgements

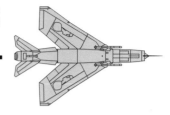

To thank everyone who helped in the preparation of this book would take several pages. Suffice to say, if you were involved thank you for helping in what I hope is the ultimate tribute to Britain's much lamented fighter. For all the people who helped me realize my ambition to become a Lightning pilot, I also offer my thanks, especially to those who said my landings were all right! To my wife and children, thank you for putting up with my absence either at work or at home. This book has been ten years in the making, and my gratitude is extended to PSL for taking on the project – something that was long overdue. My final words of appreciation are for the air and ground crews of RAF Binbrook, who gave so much. Indeed, without their help this book would never have been possible.

The author is a serving Royal Air Force fighter pilot currently flying the Mirage 2000 fighter with the French Air Force on an exchange posting. The son of a former Lightning pilot, Ian Black presently holds the distinction of becoming the RAF's last single-seat fighter pilot – a title he will retain until the Eurofighter 2000 finally enters service at the turn of the century.

A renowned aviation writer and photographer, Ian Black has produced several highly-acclaimed works over the past decade that have concentrated on the types he has flown in frontline service. All the photographs in this book were taken with Canon and Nikon cameras loaded with either Fuji or Kodak film.

Facing page:
The very 'Last of the Lightnings' are picked out in silhouette as they fly into the shallow sunset in December 1992, just days before their final retirement by British Aerospace.

This head-on view of the Lightning shows many of its unique features. Mounted on the left-hand side is the tricky access ladder, under which can be seen the gun barrel muzzles. Fitted in the circular intake is the radar bullet, and at the base of the latter is the G90 camera. Viewed from this angle, the aircraft's slab fuselage is plainly obvious.

Foreword

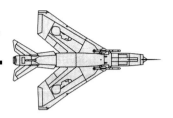

The original *The Last of the Lightnings*, published in 1996, was a tribute to a remarkable aeroplane – those who designed it, those who built it, those who serviced it and of course those who flew it. I am fortunate to have enjoyed a lifelong association with this most thoroughbred of fighters and it started at an early age. My father had flown the English Electric Lightning with 74 'Tiger' Squadron in the early 1960s and he later commanded 111 and 5 Squadrons, both of which flew Lightnings. He also taught pilots from the Royal Saudi Air Force to fly the Lightning during a spell as Chief Flying Instructor of the Lightning Operational Conversion Unit.

Showmanship at its best. My father, who was then Officer Commanding 111 Squadron, leads a diamond nine of Lightnings over a sleepy Suffolk village some 35 years ago. Flying the two-seat T4, he is surrounded by F3s in their sleek new bare-metal finish with freshly painted black and yellow tail fins. At that time the F3 was the RAF's latest fighter and was armed with head-on Red Top missiles (the T4 has Firestreaks). The single-seaters also lack the familiar air-to-air refuelling probe that was common to most Lightnings. Also of interest are the yellow trainer bands on the upper wing surfaces of the T4.

XS451 gets airborne from RAF Coningsby in the summer of 1976. Had I known then, as a sixteen year-old budding photographer, that one day I'd become a Lightning pilot – or indeed that twenty-five years later this very aircraft would be flying in private hands – I'd have bought a roll of colour film instead! But then isn't hindsight a wonderful thing? An atmospheric shot, nonetheless.

The many hours I spent watching my father fly this charismatic machine took up much of my childhood. He was an exceptional fighter pilot and it is him I have to thank for giving me the inspiration for this book. I recall one day he came home for lunch dressed in his flying suit and told me he was going to be flying later that afternoon. I asked him if he could do a steep climb after take off. 'I'll see' he replied.

Grabbing my trusty steed I rushed to the airfield crash gate and waited impatiently for my father, as little boys do. Right on time I could hear the growl of two Rolls-Royce Avons approaching as a lone, silver single-seat F1a taxied into view, canopy down, wing flaps dangling. I waved frantically at the pilot who was trussed up in his flying regalia and wearing a black and yellow Mk1 'bone dome'. I knew who it was. My father always wore his 111 Squadron helmet despite the newer styles then in vogue. He

waved back at the assembled crowd, but secretly I knew he was waving just at me.

With no other aircraft cleared to land, he lined up on the piano keys and pushed the throttles forward. The nose of the aircraft nodded down under the strain of the two powerful Avons screaming away. As the brakes came off the Lightning leapt forward pursued by a huge streak of orange and red flame issuing from the top jet pipe. Goose bumps covered me and my whole body shook. As the silver machine rushed down the runway it lifted slightly, retracted its wheels and held its attitude momentarily before rotating around the same axis and pitching upwards, cobra-like into the blue. A shimmering heat haze marked where it had once been and a silver dart pointed towards where it was heading. Straight into the vertical, riding on a column of raw power, it left the stunned Norfolk countryside below. The assembled crowd was suitably impressed. No one

10

was ever more proud of his father than me. George Black – Lightning pilot extraordinary. What more could a young boy ask?

Twenty years passed until I, too, sat alone in this magical metal monster, strapped to the ultimate fun machine. Rushing down Binbrook's runway with my destiny in both hands, it was tempting to perform a 'rote' on every flight. The Lightning begged you to do it and no other fighter brought out that 'fighting spirit' in a pilot.

Every air force has its elite type of aircraft and the Lightning's reign was longer than any fighter I know of. In the sixties it reigned supreme; in the seventies it was outclassed but not outperformed; by the eighties a resurgence of interest put the Lightning back on the map. Phantoms came and went, Tornado's arrived, Harriers jumped and Jaguars growled, but the Lightning always excelled, excited and performed.

Fortuitously, groups of people have perpetuated the Lightning's memory long after its retirement from active service. Two aircraft (XR728 and XS904) are kept in a serviceable state at Bruntingthorpe, Leicestershire, and regularly perform fast reheat runs. Brothers Chris and Richard Norris along with Hugh Trevor can be

Glory days: the F6 was a much heavier and less agile aircraft than the F3. Now retired, XR728 performs fast reheat runs at Bruntingthorpe.

justifiably proud of their efforts. Also in the UK, Tony Hulls has done a fantastic job keeping T5, XS458, in 'flying' condition, again performing regular high-speed taxi-runs at its Cranfield base. At the Lightning's last lair, Binbrook, Charles Ross keeps F6, XR724, in a taxiable state. Across the pond, Andrew Brodie and his team are close to realising their dream. They have worked tirelessly to put T5, XS422, back where she belongs – in the sky.

Finally, the jewel in the crown of the Lightning legend goes to Thunder City based in Cape Town, South Africa. Fronted by the larger-than-life Mike Beachy Head, Thunder City has truly kept the dream alive. Indeed, Mike has succeeded and exceeded where others have failed. He is now the proud owner of three airworthy Lightnings with a fourth waiting in the wings. Without wishing to steal his thunder (you can read Mike's inspiring Lightning story later in this book), Lightning fans owe him an incalculable debt for perpetuating the dream. If it had not been for him, then younger generations would have to be content with static museum exhibits, metal ghosts of awesome potential. If there was ever a flying machine that belonged in the sky, then the Lightning is it. Ripping the air with its vertical twinjets, it is the epitome of the slender bond between man and machine, an extreme adrenaline rush in every sense of the word. Those that have been privileged to fly her are the fortunate ones. In an age now governed by computers and fly-by-wire, there never will be such a charismatic jet again. The Lightning always was – and always will be – the ultimate jet fighter.

Ian Black
York, September 2002

In South African skies: Thunder City's F6, XR773, resplendent in air defence grey, August 2002.

When viewed from head-on, the Lightning takes on a stalky appearance, its cranked wing very much in evidence. Readily apparent from this shot is the aircraft's massive bolt-on underwing refuelling probe, and the minute gap left between the former and the cranked cockpit access ladder.

Often erroneously reported as having been scrapped in the early 1970s, pre-production Lightning XG313 is now preserved at the Royal Saudi Air Force (RSAF) base at Dhahran. It was originally delivered to the region in the late 1960s for use as a ground trainer, and following its retirement from this role, it sat abandoned on the airfield for a number of years. Finally rescued and restored sometime in the mid-1980s, it now takes pride of place along with a former F.52 (F.2) and T.54 (T.4) in a small aviation museum inside the large RSAF base.

CHAPTER 1

History

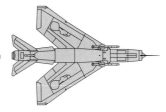

The Lightning's genesis began no sooner than peace had been declared at the end of the Second World War in 1945. Despite the fact that the government deemed manned supersonic flight too dangerous, the race was on to produce a supersonic aircraft. Britain was not alone, collaborating closely with France and the United States pushing the frontiers of technology to achieve the objective – a manned supersonic interceptor. The government was wary of the pace of change in the rapidly developing world of high speed flight. As early as 1946 they cancelled the Miles M.52, a project that would have produced an aircraft capable of flying at 1,000 mph in level flight at 36,000 ft. They believed it was simply too dangerous, and didn't have the heart to ask pilots to fly it. Instead they considered the use of a converted Mosquito bomber to drop models of these high performance aircraft from high altitude to test any new theories. This was the era of the 'Right Stuff', where test pilots were constantly stepping into the unknown, and beyond.

It is therefore somewhat paradoxical that in early 1947 English Electric (EE) was awarded a study contract for the production of an aircraft to fulfil a supersonic specification similar to that of the recently expired M.52. Chief Engineer of the EE team, W. E. W. 'Teddy' Petter, had begun sketching ideas for a supersonic aircraft the previous year, and from the outset, his drawings were for an aircraft with highly-swept wings in the region of 60° – essential in delaying the onset of compressibility at high speed. Powering this radical airframe were a

pair of engines strong enough to sustain Mach speeds. Additionally, a small frontal area was needed to keep induced drag to a minimum, vital as induced drag increases to the square of the speed. His decision to embody a twin-engined layout, but still retain a reduced frontal area, led to the prototype P.1's unique 'double stack' arrangement – some 40 years later the Lightning was still affectionately called the 'Vertical Twin Jet' by GCI (Ground Controlled Intercept) controllers.

So it was with this design that Petter confidently approached the Ministry of Supply (MoS) in early 1947 with his proposal for a supersonic aircraft. By March of that year USAAF Capt Charles 'Chuck' Yeager had exceeded Mach 1.0 in the Bell X-1, and this event prompted the MoS to issue Experimental Requirement 103, which called for a research aircraft capable of exploring transonic and low supersonic speeds up to Mach 1.5 – thus, the Lightning was born.

At this early stage, perhaps the greatest difficulty facing EE was in deciding whether the prototype should have a high T-tail or a low-mounted tailplane – the latter arrangement bordered on the unknown aerodynamically, as no one had, up to this point, fitted the horizontal tail surfaces below the level of the wings. In February 1950 'Teddy' Petter left to join Follands, where he started work on the diminutive Gnat. Two months later on 1 April, EE was awarded a contract to build three aircraft, comprising two flying prototypes and a single static airframe. Taking over where Petter left off were Ray

Creasey – the company's Chief Aerodynamicist – and F. W. Page, who assumed the now-vacant position of Chief Engineer. Additionally, in that same year the Fairey aircraft company was also awarded a contract to build a supersonic aircraft in the form of the Fairey Delta FD.2, which later went on to set the world speed record at 1,132 mph in 1956.

The major difference between the two machines was that unlike the Fairey Delta FD.2, which was a pure research vehicle, the EE P.1 was designed from the outset to have frontline fighter potential, being designed to withstand loads of 7g and have provision for armament. With the layout of the EE P.1 now finalized, concern was still being expressed by scientists at RAE Farnborough as to the prudence of the aircraft's low-mounted tailplane, which had been selected in order to prevent pitch up at transonic speeds – a common fault with T-tailed designs. Wind tunnel test had shown that a high T-tail produced pitch up, with the ensuing blanking of the tail surfaces by the fuselage resulting in a 'super

stall' – a disastrous chain of events in a combat scenario. Therefore, in order to confirm RAE suspicions, an independent company in the form of Short Bros & Harland of Belfast was awarded a contract to build a subsonic research aircraft capable of both interchangeable wing sweep angles and either a low-mounted or T-tail assembly.

Designated the SB.5, this one-off aircraft performed its maiden flight in December 1952, fitted with the T-tail. With its fixed undercarriage and single engine it was, as initially predicted to be, a difficult machine to fly, but within twelve months of its initial flight it had a representative 60° wing sweep and the low-mounted tail of the P.1. As it transpired, the Short SB.5 proved an unnecessary addition to an already charged development programme, but it did, however, bring to light the problem of lateral wing rocking at circuit speed due to an irregular breakdown of airflow from one wing to the other. A simple notch in the leading edge proved to be a simple and effective cure.

The SB.5 was also utilized by EE's Chief Test

'Plugging' in the 'burners just one last time in December 1992. Whilst the aircraft accelerates quickly away from the Hawk photo-chase, the number one reheat produces a classic supersonic diamond shock wave. XP693 was owned and operated by British Aerospace (and its forebears) throughout its entire flying life.

Still looking shiny and new some 25 years after its first flight, XP693 cruises effortlessly at 34,000 ft, high above a solid overcast sky. It is being flown here by company test pilot Keith Hartley.

Pilot, Wg Cdr 'Bee' Beamont, in order to get some hands-on experience in a platform not too dissimilar to the proposed P.1. Indeed, shortly after the first photographs were released of Britain's most secret fighter, some of its details were inadvertently given away through references to the SB.5. Understandably, the whole P.1 project was cloaked in a veil of secrecy at the time, dictating that early photographs of the aeroplane taken at Boscombe Down had to be re-touched in order to obliterate the wing shape clearly visible by the shadow it cast under the summer sun. Unfortunately, a spokesman was quoted at the same time saying that 'the SB.5 bore a similar wing shape to that of the P.1'.

With 'Teddy' Petter now working for Folland, F. W. Page led the development team as it broke new ground aeronautically, often entering into areas where no data even existed. The company had gone from the subsonic Canberra to the Mach 2+ Lightning in one jump. At that time no one was really sure what structural loads would be imposed on an airframe at supersonic speeds, and the potential problems facing EE's engineers were further compounded by the radical 60° wing sweep

and highly-stressed all-moving tailplane. The fact that the Lightning was still in service nearly three decades later bears testament to the fact that the designers fortunately got it right from the start.

With so many new areas being broached at once, a simple 'off the shelf' policy had to be adopted for the choice of engine(s). With this criterion firmly in mind, Petter therefore chose two Armstrong Siddeley Sapphire Sa.5 turbojets, each rated at 8,100 lbs of dry thrust. The preferred choice was the Rolls-Royce Avon, but at the time sufficient stocks of this engine were unavailable. Radical thinking was called for when it came to deciding on the engine layout, and eventually a unique arrangement that saw the powerplants staggered one on top of the other was chosen. The big advantage of this layout was that the P.1 now had twin engines, but boasted just a solitary small fuselage air intake. Thanks to the combined thrust of these powerplants, the P.1 would be capable of achieving supersonic flight without having to resort to the use of reheat, and thus deplete its already meagre fuel reserves. Another plus point of the staggered design was the almost non-existent asymmetric thrust problems – a big advantage in the event of an engine failure. Asymmetric thrust problems had plagued both the Meteor and Canberra. The only time that engine failure became a serious concern in the Lightning was during the take-off roll, as should the lower engine fail, the resulting downward momentum on the nose made rotation difficult.

Although many new research aircraft were being flown in Britain at this time, none were as radical as the P.1. Whilst the prototype was nearing final completion, experiments with powered controls where being successfully undertaken in a Halifax bomber, and such was the positive nature of the results being attained, EE decided to incorporate this radical new equipment into the P.1 – it operated alongside an artificial feel system. At this stage little consideration was given to fuel capacity, which is a little surprising given that the aircraft that was being designed for supersonic flight with or without the use of reheat. The main fuselage was therefore left free of fuel tanks, and the main wing torsion box utilized as an integral tank instead. In reality, there was no available space for fuel in the fuselage as the

ingenious, but complex, bifurcated air duct system that allowed equal amounts of air to reach both engines from a single air intake effectively blocked all available space. Sited just behind the main wing torsion box were the main undercarriage legs, these being longer than similar items fitted to most other contemporary fighters in order to compensate for the high nose-up attitude adopted by the P.1 on take-off and landing. Due to its relatively thin wing the aircraft's main gear and tyres were very large in diameter, and inflated to high pressure. In order to keep the intake unobstructed the nosewheel would have to lie flat, and was therefore built to castor through 90° after retraction.

The Defence White Paper of 1954 gave passing mention to a supersonic interceptor of British design that would fly that year, but gave no clue as to its identity, or manufacturer. By the spring of 1954 the P.1 was ready, being moved from EE's Warton site, in Lancashire, to the more suitable long runway at the RAF's test airfield at Boscombe Down, in Wiltshire. The initial taxy trials and maiden flight would be performed by Wg Cdr 'Bee' Beamont. A

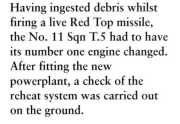

Having ingested debris whilst firing a live Red Top missile, the No. 11 Sqn T.5 had to have its number one engine changed. After fitting the new powerplant, a check of the reheat system was carried out on the ground.

A typical winter's day in England – dank and miserable from ground level to 3,000 ft, then clear above – provides the backdrop for this shot of Binbrook flagship XR728 'JS', seen here preparing to recover back to base.

celebrated and renowned wartime pilot who had become the first Englishman to officially go supersonic in 1948 whilst test flying an American F-86 Sabre at Edwards Air Force Base, in California, 'Bee' worked closely with the EE design team, staying with the Lightning project from start to finish – a period of some 20 years – and undoubtedly must be credited with ensuring that the aeroplane boasted such fine handling qualities.

After a series of high- and low-speed taxi tests, which proved the aircraft's braking system and brake parachute, an initial 'hop' was made on 24 July 1954 to confirm the aircraft's 'unstick' speed of 125 knots. From these hops it was ascertained that the P.1 had a slight tendency to weathercock in a crosswind as the brake chute deployed – a trait that was to remain with the Lightning throughout its life. After a thorough systems check, the P.1 was readied for its maiden flight.

On 4 August, 'Bee' took off from Boscombe Down's long runway, taking the aircraft up to 15,000 ft and Mach 0.85. Afterwards he stated that the P.1 flew beautifully, and had remained aerodynamically stable. The only problems encountered was radio failure and a slight over-gearing of the controls. The first flight was not, however, without incident, for after losing his radio, 'Bee' discovered that the weather conditions were deteriorating rapidly, and he was forced to sneak his way back into the Boscombe Down circuit as the cloud base had lowered to 300 ft since take-off.

After the usual post-first-flight checks, the P.1 was flown again on 6 August, and during the sortie it actually achieved Mach 1.0, although the pilot was totally unaware of this until the following day when the instrument results were examined. Although the test programme was progressing at a fast pace, the P.1 had not achieved ten hours total flight time, and was therefore unable to participate in the annual Farnborough Airshow, held in early September. Later that month the aircraft returned to Warton to continue its evaluation. As the higher Mach numbers

Literally riding 'piggy back',
two camouflaged Lightnings sit
in close echelon formation.
The extremely cramped
cockpit conditions endured by
the pilot, who was literally
shoehorned into his aircraft
back at Binbrook, are
graphically illustrated in this
photograph.

were achieved, it became obvious that the fin was too small to provide adequate directional stability, and this fault was duly cured on production Lightnings through the fitment of a larger fin area.

With the aircraft's Armstrong Siddeley Sapphire engines still only rated in dry power, EE's engineers felt that it was an acceptable risk to implement a crude form of fixed-nozzle reheat system in an effort to further increase thrust levels. This would raise power output by ten to twelve per cent in reheat, but in the dry power range reduce it by 50 per cent, thus giving the aircraft a 'no single-engine envelope', deemed an acceptable risk. In the end, at speeds of Mach 1.52 it was felt that directional stability had dropped to a level below which it was unsafe to continue.

By the end of July 1955 the second prototype – designated the P.1A – had flown, this aircraft differing from its predecessor by having American-style toe brakes and guns. Even before the P.1's first flight, the Air Ministry was so impressed with EE's work that it issued a contract to produce a dedicated

fighter version, designated the P.1B. Despite its similarities to the P.1, the P.1B was an altogether different beast, being designed from the outset to carry a Ferranti AI.23 AIRPASS (Airborne Interception Radar Pilot Attack System) radar in a pressurized conical centre body housed within the redesigned inclined-shock intake. Armament would consist of either two Firestreak missiles on external pylons and twin cannon, or cannon and a rocket pack housed in the same interchangeable weapons pack as used for the Firestreak missiles.

With the availability of the Rolls-Royce Avon Mk 201 engines, EE had to drastically modify the fuselage shape in order to accommodate the larger four-stage, reheated, powerplants. The canopy was also modified, and gave rise to a dorsal spine which not only housed much vital equipment, but also served to further improve lateral stability. The spine also included the engine starter control unit, and its associated iso-propyl-nitrate liquid tank. The nose wheel was made to retract into the fuselage without folding, and an underfuselage fuel tank was to be incorporated in later marks. Since the P.1's first flight, 'Bee' Beamont had also asked the designers to try to incorporate a one-piece bubble canopy for the aircraft. This would have been a tremendous bonus. However, with little knowledge of the pressures and temperatures associated with high-speed flight, the idea had to be abandoned.

The day of the P.1B's maiden flight proved momentous, as not only did 'Bee' take it supersonic, but the Minister of Defence, Mr Duncan Sandys, announced his plans for the future defence of Great Britain in the form of the now infamous White Paper of 4 April 1957. Had the Lightning programme not been so far advanced, and generally progressing so well, it too would have been axed like so many other projects of the period. Indeed, despite its reprieve, the outlook for the manned fighter looked bleak.

Nonetheless, the P.1B's first flight went smoothly, it initially flew with a solid metal radome but no ventral fuel tank. However, celebrations at the EE factory must have been tinged with apprehension in the knowledge that Britain's aircraft industry had been thrown into disarray thanks to the Sandys announcement. Following P.1B XA847, a further two hybrid machines in the form of XA853 and XA856 duly entered the test programme. Now that the aircraft's potential had at last been realized, the MoS ordered 20 additional pre-production machines that would each be given a specific development task to perform, thus speeding up the type's introduction into frontline service.

On 23 October 1958 the P.1B XA847 was officially christened the Lightning during a ceremony held at RAE Farnborough. A suitably-polished aircraft having a bottle of champagne broken across its nose by the then Chief of the Air Staff, Marshal of the Royal Air Force Sir Dermot Boyle – from then on it was simply known as the Lightning, other names muted at the time for the EE fighter having included Excalibur. A company press release issued to mark the event stated that 'the Lightning would remain in squadron service for up to ten years with the RAF' – how pessimistic this proved to be.

Within one month of the naming ceremony,

Fully-armed with its quota of two Red Tops, this F.6 waits at readiness for the call to 'scramble', its pilot already strapped in.

Wg Cdr Beamont had put the first P.1B past Mach 2.0, and although the RAF requirement stipulated that the aircraft only had to be capable of Mach 1.7, it soon became clear that the Lightning had plenty of power in reserve to push it well beyond this figure – indeed, tests had shown that parity in the total thrust versus drag line equation would not occur until Mach 2.2 was reached. XA847 was the aircraft used by 'Bee' Beamont to pass Mach 2.0 (on 25 November 1958), and thus become the first British aircraft to fly at twice the speed of sound. Shortly after this flight he wrote to the MoS emphasizing that the RAF now had a Mach 2.0 fighter, but it must increase the aircraft's internal fuel capacity to make it truly effective. Sadly, little was done over the next five years to rectify this problem.

By the end of April 1958 the first of the 20 pre-

Generations apart – the Wattisham wing in the early 1960s. The shot is by Peter M. Warren, a local photographer who produced some lovely work.

production Lightnings had made its maiden flight, again with Wg Cdr Beamont at the controls. This time the sortie took place from Samlesbury, located a short distance away from Warton, and by September 1959 all 20 pre-production machines had taken to the air. Now fitted with Avon RA.24R engines with four-stage reheat that pushed their individual thrust rating up to 14,430 lbs, these pre-production aeroplanes were instrumental in both the evolution and service introduction of the Lightning.

Stability problems were still afflicting the P.1Bs at this late stage in the fighter's development, so one aircraft (XG310) was fitted with an increased area (+30 per cent) fin, which was made standard on all

later service Lightnings. The other aircraft each carried out various aspects of the development trials programme, ranging from hydraulic systems checks to sorting out the aeroplane's handling characteristics and testing its weapons systems. The contract to develop the Lightning radar had been awarded as early as 1954 to Edinburgh-based defence company Ferranti, who in turn fitted a former RAF Dakota with a nose-mounted AI.23 to help in testing the new AIRPASS system – the aircraft flew from nearby Turnhouse. In addition to the radar, the Dakota also boasted a suitably-modified cockpit display, replete with all the associated instruments to accompany the AI.23

LAST OF THE LIGHTNINGS

including a radar display, hand-controller and attack sight. Thanks in part to the hybrid aircraft, the AIRPASS system went on to become the world's first monopulse radar to achieve frontline service.

After initial trials had been completed, the radar was installed in a modified Canberra BI.8, followed by several of the development P.1Bs. One Lightning, XG312, was allocated to Ferranti for exclusive use on radar development work, although all trials were flown from Warton as the runway at Turnhouse was too short. This particular aircraft last flew in 1966, having clocked up a mere 300 hours – about par for the remaining 19 development machines. By the mid-1960s most of the surviving development aircraft had ceased flying. Four had been lost, two of which had fallen victim to undercarriage problems, one to hydraulic failure and the remaining aircraft to an inflight fire.

Although the development phase had now been successfully completed, a number of problems had beset the pre-production fleet during the period of the trials. One of the primary headaches constantly afflicting EE was the logistical nightmare the company faced in supporting up to 20 new aircraft dotted around the UK on various trials. Indeed, so bad was the problem that the whole fleet was grounded on numerous occasions through a lack of spares.

Nevertheless, the soundness of the design carried the day, and the first true fighter airframe – F.1 XM134 – successfully completed its maiden flight on 29 October 1959. A further 19 F.1s were subsequently built, although the last aircraft never flew, as it was retained at Warton as a static fatigue specimen. Two months after the first flight of the production F.1, the RAF received its premier example of the Lightning in the form of XG334, this late pre-production aircraft being delivered to the Central Fighter Establishment's Air Fighting Development Squadron (AFDS) at Coltishall, in Norfolk. This was followed shortly after by two further aircraft – XG335 and XG336 – which arrived just before the end of 1959. The task of the AFDS was to develop tactics and operational procedures prior to the type entering RAF service.

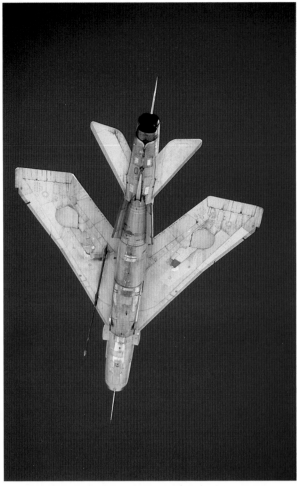

XR727 'BH' prepares for its last ever flight – a transit from Binbrook to Wildenrath, where it was to be employed as an airfield decoy. Flown by Flt Lt Ian Hollingworth, whose name appeared under the cockpit, it survived for several years before being scrapped.

At the same time the unit operated a number of other fighters including the Hunter and Javelin, plus a handful of Meteor hacks. Although the AFDS was the first official recipient of the Lightning, the honour of operating the frontline F.1s went to No. 74 'Tiger' Sqn, who moved to Coltishall in the summer of 1959. They were destined to become the only unit to operate the F.1, their first aircraft arriving at the Norfolk fighter station in June 1960.

Now that the Lightning was in the throes of entering frontline service, attention turned to the aircraft's export potential. The story of the aircraft's export success, or lack of it, is worthy of a book in itself. The Lightning was a fighter with a potential for worldwide export success for Britain, a potential that was sadly never capitalised upon. At the beginning of 1958 the US Air Force was in the

A 28 mm lens and a low ground angle combine to exaggerate the bulbous nose profile of the T5 trainer.

process of introducing the Lockheed F-104 Starfighter into service, an aircraft in the Mach 2.0 class that had first flown in February 1954. The Lockheed fighter had a troubled gestation that resulted in the entire fleet being grounded following a series of crashes attributed to engine failure. The F-104 also had a poor serviceability record and a combat range of around 600 miles. Due to a combination of these factors, it was quickly judged by USAF senior officers to be a less than ideal platform for guarding the vast American continent, and it therefore came as no surprise when, just two years after its introduction, the F-104A was withdrawn from frontline service.

Lockheed was suddenly left with an aircraft that its primary customer didn't want, having geared up for large-scale production. In many respects the F-104 was in a class of its own by 1959, as it held both the world altitude and speed records, having reached a staggering 103,395 ft and Mach 2.4. It was, however, less than a match for the Lightning in many respects – having fought the F-104 in air combat, I can confidently state without too much fear of contradiction that the Lightning was a vastly superior platform.

In Europe the market was ripe for new-generation

fighters to replace the vast stocks of subsonic types then in service with NATO countries who were desperate to upgrade. In the Eastern Bloc, the highly-acclaimed MiG-21 Fishbed was just becoming a threat, outclassing everything except the Lightning. On paper, therefore, EE's superior interceptor appeared to have the market cornered, but the company's sales pitch to the West Germans (who were leading the NATO purchase) came to nothing as the British government were pushing the Saunders Roe SR.53 'rocket plane'. Had the Germans procured the Lightning, then there was every possibility that many other NATO F-104 users would have followed suit. By the early 1960s the next potential overseas customer appeared to be the Indian Air Force – indeed, at one point it looked as if No. 74 Sqn would lose all its F.1s to the Indians, who were keen to make an immediate purchase – but the deal fell through principally because of the fighter's price tag.

Like any new aircraft entering service, the Lightning's early days in the frontline were plagued with major technical problems – No. 74 Sqn's F.1s were on occasions grounded for up to three months whilst manufacturer's modifications were carried out. Looking through my father's log book (he was one of the first pilots to join No. 74 Sqn), he flew just 180 hours between 1961 and '63, the bulk of this time comprising formation aerobatics. Seldom were the sorties purely radar work or air combat, and to keep current most pilots flew the Hunter T.7 attached to the squadron or the Station Flight Meteor T.7. Early solos were accompanied by Hunter chase aircraft flown by an experienced pilot who could hopefully talk you through any problems that arose whilst in flight. Initially, all new Lightning pilots were required to have flown a minimum of 1,000 hours in jet aircraft before being considered for a posting onto the RAF's most prestigious fighter. However, this stipulation was soon relaxed when the RAF discovered that the aircraft possessed excellent handling qualities.

The transition from a subsonic to a supersonic RAF Fighter Command had been relatively painless, but the need for a two-seat trainer variant was

Almost at the end of its life, and showing signs of age, F.6 XS935 displays its squared-tipped fin – characteristic of all later Lightnings – and distinctive No. 5 Sqn markings. The vertical engine layout is also clearly visible, as is the silver band around the jet pipes which held the cabling for the brake parachute. Dangling beneath the fuselage from a T-key, the small red and white flag indicates that the ground lock for the arrestor hook is fitted.

nevertheless recognized as early as 1957. The first prototype flew in May 1959, and was virtually identical to the F.1, with the exception of the forward fuselage, which was widened to accommodate the side-by-side seating arrangement – similar to that found in the Hunter T.7. The layout worked well in the new T.4, the aircraft boasting similar performance to the F.1, although it lacked the latter's cannon fitment. On 1 October the prototype T.4 was lost over the Irish Sea when its fin broke off during supersonic high-rate rolls, the latter having suffered structural failure. Fortunately, the pilot escaped, and a second T.4 was airborne and continuing development flying by the end of the month. The first production T.4 trainer was delivered to the Lightning Conversion Squadron (LCS) at Middleton St George in December 1961, although its stay was to be short-lived as it soon returned to EE for a complete rework of the

Despite the unusual overwing tank arrangement causing a high-drag penalty on the normally 'slick' F.6, the aircraft could still rapidly climb high into the troposphere thanks to the abundance of excess thrust available from its twin Avons.

hydraulic pipes in the number one engine bay – it was reissued to the LCS in July 1962, and by October of that year the unit had seven T.4s on strength.

Whilst the LCS was building up its strength, two squadrons (Nos 56 and 111) had received the latest F.1A variant of the Lightning at Wattisham, in Suffolk, between late 1960 and early 1961. This new mark differed from the F.1 through the fitment of a detachable in-flight refuelling probe, which was located under the left wing and extended as far forward as the cockpit. Fuselage cable ducting was also externally visible on the F.1A, covering an extensive wiring loom, whilst internally, the fighter now also had a UHF radio as standard equipment. Not surprisingly then, the two Wattisham squadrons spent much of their time with the F.1A practising and developing air-to-air refuelling techniques.

No. 56 Sqn earned a brief spell of fame when it was selected to be the official RAF Fighter Command aerobatic display team for 1963. Starting their work-up in February of that year, the team was short-lived and only performed at five shows. Known as the 'Firebirds', they did, however, put the

Lightning 'on the map' with its breathtaking displays capitalising on the aeroplane's sheer power in every sense. Whilst No. 56 Sqn stole the limelight at airshows like Paris, 'Treble One' was busy discovering the Lightning's air-to-air refuelling capabilities – a necessity with the aircraft's notoriously meagre fuel reserves. Whilst operating the F.1A No. 111 Sqn had more than its fair share of losses, due mainly to technical faults – indeed, after losing their fourth aircraft, additional replacements were added to the squadron strength through the employment of two ex-No. 74 Sqn F.1s. These aircraft differed so much from the latest variant that only more experienced squadron pilots were allowed to fly them. In reality they rarely flew on a day to day basis, spending most of their time assigned to QRA (Quick Reaction Alert) duties – even employing the F.1 in this role was a risky business as both aircraft lacked air-to-air refuelling probes!

The next single-seat variant to enter service was the F.2, of which 44 were eventually built – the first one flew on 11 July 1961. This version was essentially a refined F.1A, outwardly differing little from the early mark save for a small air intake on the spine, which was used to power the aircraft's standby DC generator. Internally, however, the story was rather different as the F.2 was fitted with partial OR 946 instrumentation, although it lacked the novel 'strip' speed display fitted to later aircraft. A Liquid Oxygen (LOX) breathing system was used for the first time, and the Lightning also now had a highly-effective offset TACAN (Tactical Air Navigation) display. This allowed the pilot to fictitiously move the TACAN beacon from its ground position to a location of his choice, thus making recoveries into non-TACAN equipped bases possible. Finally, the Lightning was fitted with a fully variable reheat system in the shape of two Rolls-Royce Avon 210 engines. Despite the RAF's order for 44 F.2s, only 36 entered frontline service, with the rest being either used for trials work or exported to Saudi Arabia.

The two squadrons destined to receive the F.2 were Nos 19 and 92, both having been former Hunter operators – indeed, the latter had recently

provided Fighter Command with their official display team in the form of the 'Blue Diamonds'. The initial work-up for the two units was conducted using a pool of T.4 trainers allocated to Leconfield to ease the smooth transition from the comparatively sedate Hunter F.6 to the Mach 2.0+ Lightning F.2. By the summer of 1963 both squadrons had received their full complement of F.2s at Leconfield, and after two years of flying from their Yorkshire base, both units were transferred to RAF Germany – No. 92 Sqn was initially based at Geilenkirchen and No. 19 at Gutersloh, but by 1968 the former had also moved to the latter base due to its strategic location near the East German border.

April 1964 saw the service debut of the next frontline Lightning variant to enter service – the F.3. The most potent of the breed to date, it differed greatly from the earlier marks thanks to the fitment of the ultimate Avon engine in the shape of the Mk

301. Further adding to its status as a true second generation fighter, the F.3 incorporated state-of-the-art technology within its weapons system. The aircraft was fitted with the much-improved AI.23B radar, which was optimized for the latest RAF air-to-air missile in the form of the all-aspect Red Top. Additionally, the fin was enlarged and given a square top, a characteristic of all later Lightning marks – this had been trialled some years earlier on a development aircraft, but was first adopted on the F.3.

Notwithstanding the fitting of the Red Top missile, the reality of a pure head-on capability was still somewhat vague. With many early difficulties encountered, the Firestreak pack was often used. A major bonus of the Lightning was its self-contained weapons pack which could be quickly changed on the ground with no requirement to bolt on or add different stores pylons. The Red Top had a long

Fittingly preserved in authentic No. 56 Sqn colours at the entrance to RAF Akrotiri, in Cyprus, F.6 XS929 formerly served with the unit on the island between 1973 and 1975. Delivered by the author to its final resting place on 25 May 1988 (just days before the end of Lightning operations) it was returned to its original silver colour scheme prior to being mounted on its plinth.

In order to create a more realistic decoy, this particular F.2A was 'trussed up' to look like a Soviet Su-22 Fitter – quite what a Soviet aircraft would have been doing at RAF Laarbruch I never did quite fathom out! With the addition of Hunter drop tanks and a shortened fin, it produced a passable double.

gestation period, and never achieved the reliability of the earlier Firestreak. A major drawback with the F.3 was its lack of air-to-air cannon, and this factor probably made this version of the Lightning the first pure missile-equipped fighter to enter service with the RAF. Despite lacking a gun, and the Red Top's continued reliability problems, the F.3 was the most numerous of any Lightning mark to enter service, with no less than 70 being built. It also had the distinction of being the longest-serving, the last F.3 completing its final flight in 1987.

With its almost one-to-one thrust-to-weight ratio, it was an ideal mount for both visual combat and aerobatics, and for the first time, the RAF had a fighter that could out-perform anything the USAF could put up against it. In all, 62 F.3s saw frontline service with Nos 23, 29, 56, 74 and 111 Sqns. The mid-1960s became arguably Fighter Command's most flamboyant era since its pre-war days. The Lightning was an aircraft that was loved by those who flew it throughout its long career, endearing a strong sense of national pride. Even those who had the challenging task of servicing the Lightning grew to love it, so it was hardly surprising that the aircraft became adorned in lavish – almost exotic – colour schemes that showed off unit pride. The two

Leuchars-based squadrons – Nos 23 and 74 – painted their mounts with coloured fins (white and black, respectively), and not to be outdone the Wattisham wing also adorned its factory-fresh F.3s with appropriate unit colours as they arrived at the Suffolk station. First to re-equip was No. 111 Sqn, who adopted a similar scheme to that used on their F.1As except for squaring off the yellow flash on the fin to keep it symmetrical – the RAF fin flash was also moved forward. Not to be outdone, No. 56 Sqn adopted a scheme that must have kept the unit's painters and finishers busy into the 'small hours' decorating the aircraft as they arrived from BAC. Each machine had its fin covered in a bright red and white chequer-board design, which was a radical departure from the units earlier maroon red fin and leading edge scheme. Rivalry between Lightning squadrons during this period was intense, and no doubt the OC of No. 56 Sqn was less than impressed when one of his newly-painted aircraft returned from landing away at another base with several of its white squares defaced with drawings of chess pieces emblazoned across them.

In 1965 No. 111 Sqn took their aircraft to Paris as the official RAF display team, where they flew a challenging routine that hinged on all the unit's

LAST OF THE LIGHTNINGS

aircraft being serviceable on each day of the show – led by the squadron T.4, the team performed flawlessly throughout the week-long event. The Paris event of that year was also the last time the public saw real British showmanship in the skies, as a mixed formation of nine Lightnings and seven Gnats of the new Red Arrows team performed an aerobatics routine that was never to be repeated – the RAF deemed it too costly an exercise to have a dedicated display team drawn from Fighter Command. As confidence grew with the aircraft, so more demanding profiles were flown against a range of high-flying targets including USAF Lockheed U-2 reconnaissance aircraft, which on paper looked immune to attack when cruising at their optimum operational ceiling in the upper stratosphere. However, American crews soon became accustomed to seeing Lightnings from the Wattisham wing sailing past them whilst in the process of performing a 'vis-ident'. With the introduction of high speed intercepts, fuel awareness became even more acute, and on more than one occasion Lightnings landed

back at base on fumes only. By the end of 1965 the flamboyant days of Fighter Command were over, and all Lightnings reverted to their natural metal finish adorned with a small unit crest. Shortly afterwards, No. 56 Sqn moved to its new home at RAF Akrotiri, in Cyprus, where it replaced the Javelin-equipped No. 29 Sqn, who in turn flew back to the UK to re-equip with the Lightning.

Whilst the United Kingdom Air Defence squadrons were getting to grips with the F.3, things were moving apace at Warton, with many new developments being trialled. As early as 1962, the Lightning had been displayed at Farnborough fitted with a larger ventral tank, whilst the original P.1A had already flown with a redesigned larger cambered wing. Both changes produced few penalties in terms of drag – indeed, the range was increased by 20 per cent – and handling remained virtually unchanged. In order to improve range still further, a solution was found for fitting additional external tanks to the Lightning. Because of its location, the undercarriage prevented underwing

For the best part of 25 years, Lightnings sat alert ready to defend UK airspace. Here, the Binbrook Quick Reaction Alert (QRA) hangar doors remain open so as not to impede any potential scramble. Known simply as the 'Q sheds', the hangar housed two fully-armed Lightnings that were ready to take off within five minutes of receiving the launch order, 365 days a year, 24 hours a day. The aircraft to the left was known as 'Q1' and that on the right as 'Q2'. A single 'Q' Lightning was normally launched in response to a scramble order, the second aircraft acting as a spare should the primary jet suffer a technical malfunction.

Still performing a useful role long after their flying days were over, many RAFG F.2/.2As were 'put out to grass' to act as surface decoys. Often used in station exercises, they added a touch of realism to the fictitious incidents dreamt up by the tactical planners. This unfortunate F.2A has been pushed into the corner of a wood at RAF Wildenrath with its undercarriage semi-retracted in order to simulating a crashed aircraft. It no doubt kept the rescue crews 'busy' during the exercise period.

tanks being an option, in a typically British display of ingenuity, British Aircraft Corporation (BAC, formerly EE) came up with the idea of incorporating overwing hard points which could be used to mount jettisonable fuel tanks. Trials soon proved the viability of the modification, and overwing tanks were built for squadron use.

With the maturing of the design, the Lightning now became a viable export fighter, and having missed out in Europe, the company turned its attention to the oil-rich Gulf states, and in particular Saudi Arabia. The latter's air force at that time was comprised primarily of antiquated F-86 Sabres, 16 of which had been delivered in 1958 – some of these had never entered service due to an immediate spares problem. As border violations by more modern fighters from neighbouring countries rose in frequency, it became apparent that the Royal Saudi Air Force (RSAF) was ill-equipped to see off any would-be aggressor.

BAC were quick to see a market for a complete air defence system sale to Saudi Arabia, and at short notice 'Jimmy' Dell – then deputy company test pilot – was despatched to display the Lightning to the

then Minister of Defence. RAF Lightnings were staging back through neighbouring Bahrain at the time, and provision was made for the loan of a 'markingless' F.2 to BAC. There is little doubt that Dell's sparkling display persuaded the Saudis to procure the Lightning, and what followed was Britain's biggest ever overseas export order – not only would they purchase the Lightning, but also the infrastructure to help keep it in service for almost 20 years. The project was code-named *Magic Palm*, and the massive venture provided lucrative employment in the Middle East for thousands of British workers. Prior to the delivery of the latest spec Lightnings to the RSAF, the Saudis took charge of a number of former RAF aircraft bought back by BAC. Initially five F.52s were delivered, with a further two T.54s being supplied for conversion training and a single non-flying development batch aircraft employed in the ground-instructional role. Additionally, one F.52 was retained in the UK by the Saudi Support Flight at Warton. These early airframes were basically F.2s and T.4s modified slightly to cope with the extreme heat of the Gulf, and they were immediately put to work showing the flag, and generally restoring public confidence through a succession of flypasts and demonstrations.

The main export order was for 34 single-seater and six two-seat trainers, to be designated F.53 and T.55 respectively, and these proved to be the most capable Lightnings ever built. Not only did they have the ability to carry a vast array of weapons for both the air defence and ground attack roles, but they could also tote a reconnaissance pack designed for either day or night missions. Additional hardpoints underneath the outer wings allowed a total of four 1,000-lb 'iron' bombs to be carried – a fitment never adopted by the fighter-optimized RAF Lightning force. Quickly following the Saudi lead, neighbouring Kuwait ordered twelve single-seat F.53s and two T.55 two-seaters. At last it looked like the fighter would enjoy a degree of export success, just as the Meteor and Hunter had before it. However, further export orders were not forthcoming, principally because the British government badly-timed their announcement that the Lightning was soon be replaced in the air defence role by the American-built F-4 Phantom II.

Complementing the F.3 in RAF service was the T.5 which first flew from BAC's factory at Filton,

with Jimmy Dell at the controls – the first two prototypes were in fact converted from production T.4s. Mirroring the earlier loss of the first T.4 prototype, Dell and his observer were forced to eject from the second T.5 through yet another fin failure.

Like the early twin-seat Lightnings, the T.5 was fully operational in every respect, although the cockpit layout differed markedly between the two variants – the T.4 had been built with a centre console housing a throttle quadrant for the instructor in the right-hand seat, whilst the T.5 had a throttle box on both the left and right-hand cockpit walls – this led to all instructors developing ambidextrous piloting skills, flying with the left hand on the stick and the right-hand on the throttles. This odd arrangement led to several amusing incidents where pilots in the right-hand seat became confused with the layout and 'pushed' when they meant to 'pull', and vice versa. Generally, however, after a few hours in the right-hand seat handling the T.5 posed few problems.

Conversion onto the Lightning was performed by No. 226 Operational Conversion Unit (OCU), who operated a mixture of F.1s, F.1As, T.4s and T.5s standardized into three flights. The unit also held the

John Carter brings LTF T.5 XV328 in close for the benefit of the camera. Fitted with a finless Red Top training missile, the aircraft's forward fuselage shows signs of recent repair. Using the aeroplane's excellent autopilot, the easiest way to photograph other aircraft was to engage this system and let other aircraft formate on you. This particular aircraft was half of the final order for two T.5s placed with BAC in 1965 (XV329 was the other airframe), and it initially went into service with No. 29 Sqn at Wattisham as 'Z' in April 1967. By the time it was sold off to Arnold Glass in June 1988, it had flown 3,021 hours.

31

Looking vertically up at a 'Diamond Nine' of Lightnings, the sun's rays scattering in all directions off the canopy of the photo-chase T.5.

shadow 'number plate' of No. 145 Sqn. As the operational squadrons converted onto the F.3, sufficient F.1As became available to equip a single flight with these aircraft, and several two-seat T.4s, for the basic training role, whilst a second advanced training flight utilized all the T.5s. At times the unit had up to 35 Lightnings on strength, and with the F.1's final replacement on the OCU, several older airframes became free for use with the Target Facilities Flights (TFFs). Others were simply scrapped, despite their low airframe hours. Three bases were selected for TFFs, namely Binbrook, Leuchars and Wattisham, and after the airframes had been overhauled and stripped of non-essential equipment, they were each fitted with Luneburg lens radar reflectors. This magnified the F.1's radar signature, and thus made it easier for the opposing

fighter to acquire. The establishment of the trio of TFFs removed the need for operational units to use their own fighters as targets, which has always been both a costly business and of little training value to the 'target' pilot.

The first recipient of the final version of Lightning for the RAF was No. 5 Sqn, a former Javelin operator. Designated the F.6, the aircraft could trace its origins directly back to the F.3 – indeed, the RAF were so impressed with the reports emanating from BAC during its development trials that they asked the company to convert the remaining eleven F.3s still under construction to F.6 standard. Notable differences included a large 600 gallon belly tank, increased area cambered wings and provision to carry overwing fuel tanks. Initial deliveries at first lacked the overwing hard points, but soon all F.6s were modified to incorporate this feature. For a while delivery of the latest version was slow, with production rarely exceeding three aircraft a month – a problem which forced No. 5 Sqn to initially make good the shortfall in airframes by using a Hunter T.7 partially fitted with Lightning instrumentation. However, by the spring of 1966 all aircraft had been delivered, and the gradual re-equipment of other F.3 squadrons began.

With the Cold War at its peak, the next recipient of the F.6 was Leuchars-based No. 11 Sqn, who had also been operating Javelins prior to the arrival of the Lightning – few would have believed that the squadron's association with the F.6 would span some 21 years. Once fully equipped, the unit took up the QRA tasking from No. 74 'Tiger' Sqn, who left Scotland bound for Singapore to replace the Javelins of the Far East Air Force (FEAF). Under the code name of *Exercise Hydraulic*, the unit flew first to Cyprus and then on to Singapore all in the first week of June 1967. The whole staging procedure took a full seven days, and when they arrived at their new home in the shape of RAF Tengah, they were soon declared 'operational'. Lacking the large ventral tank of the F.6, the squadron's T.5 had to complete the trip as deck cargo on a freighter, and was damaged during the transit. Whilst in the Far East the squadron took part in many notable exercises,

Day or night, Binbrook was a busy airfield right to the end. When the aircrew weren't flying the aircraft, the ground crew were fixing them. Like the pilots, the engineers operated a 24-hour shift system, and with the last night landing usually not taking place until after midnight, ground crews often worked into the early hours fixing unserviceable airframes so that they would be ready for the next day's flying.

including the one and only deployment of Lightnings to Darwin, Australia, in 1969.

Prior to the 'Tigers" disbandment, No. 5 Sqn flew out later modified F.6s in order to allow older No. 74 Sqn machines to be flown back to England for major servicing. The whole procedure took around six weeks, and ultimately less than half a dozen former No. 74 Sqn aircraft were returned to the Maintenance Unit at Leconfield. The squadron had always been somewhat 'out on a limb' being so far away from the UK, but despite this handicap, they upheld the unit's proud tradition. From a pilot's perspective, the major drawback of an FEAF posting centred around the lack of clear airspace in which to work, the small island nation being tightly hemmed in by neighbouring countries. Further adding to the operational restrictions was the lack of a flight simulator at Tengah, all pilots having to return to UK if 'sim time' was required. The only standards check carried out by the squadron took the form of an annual visit by instructors from the OCU, who had the unenviable task of trying to fly with all the unit's pilots in the sole T.5 in a hectic two-week period. In August 1971 the RAF withdrew from the

Even if you attempted to capture this image a hundred times over, only luck could produce the perfect result. Exquisitely framed by the F.3 in the foreground, Flt Lt Steve Hunt breaks away from the formation, displaying the underside of his aircraft as he does so.

Far East, and No. 74 Sqn flew its aircraft back to Cyprus, where it handed them over to No. 56 Sqn. The T.5 again returned by sea, but this time was so badly damaged in transit that it was scrapped soon after arriving back in the UK.

A major milestone occurred in the aircraft's history when the last Lightning (XS938) was delivered to the RAF in August 1967, although no sooner had it rolled off the production line than Warton commenced the conversion of F.2s to F.2A standard, which essentially saw the aircraft uprated to F.6 standard (including the fitment of the squared-off tail). This programme was to run for several years, with a total of 31 aircraft being involved in the conversion – all remaining standard F.2s stayed with their squadrons as TFF aircraft.

The end of the 1960s saw the Lightning force reach its zenith, with nine frontline squadrons plus a very large OCU operating the type. Hard to believe that no sooner had it reached its peak when the infinitely more capable, but hardly glamorous, F-4

Phantom II began to be employed in the air defence role. The writing was on the wall when No. 43 Sqn equipped with the F-4K, taking up residence at Leuchars next to the F.6 squadrons. Ironically, as it transpired the Phantom II only just outlived the Lightning, being withdrawn from service in 1992.

At its peak, the Lightning was serving concurrently in the Far East, Cyprus, Germany and the UK when the run down of the force began in 1971. As noted earlier, No. 74 Sqn relinquished its F.6s to No. 56 Sqn in Cyprus, whose F.3s in turn flew back to the UK for re-distribution to other units. The latter unit had enjoyed a long association with Cyprus, and had on more than one occasion flown Lightnings on armed combat air patrols during the Turkish/Greek crisis. Lightning pilots reported watching Turkish F-100 Super Sabres strafing targets, but were unable to do anything due to the rules of engagement which stated that they were there to protect the Sovereign Base Areas only, and refrain from getting involved in the national crisis. By the mid-1970s the Anglo-French Jaguar had begun to replace ground-attack Phantom IIs in sufficient numbers to allow the re-equipping of several Lightning squadrons with the McDonnell Douglas fighter. The F.6s of No. 56 Sqn returned to Wattisham to replace Nos 29 and 111 Sqns, who had moved north following the replacement of their F.3s by Phantom IIs – the latter unit had actually flown a number of F.6s just prior to their re-equipment to allow squadron pilots remaining in the Lightning force to convert onto type before being posted. As it transpired, No. 111 Sqn had to make do for some time with ex-Royal Navy Phantom FG.1s before sufficient FGR.2s were released. Next to go were F.6-equipped Nos 23 and 56 Sqns, who gave up their aircraft to the wing at Binbrook, which was rapidly becoming the Lightning's 'last lair'.

By 1976 the only Lightnings left abroad were the F.2As at Gutersloh, these aircraft having been issued to Nos 19 and 92 Sqns between 1968 and 1970 as replacements for their F.2s, which had in turn been sent back to their Warton birthplace for conversion to the improved spec. These were to soldier on until 1977, when No. 92 Sqn flew its last Lightnings to fighter stations in both the UK and RAF Germany to act as decoys – indeed, the distinction of performing the very last flight by an RAFG Lightning fell to No. 92 Sqn's T.4 when it flew from Gutersloh to Wildenrath on 6 April 1977 to undertake decoy duties.

Often considered by those who flew them to be the ultimate Lightnings to see RAF service, the Gutersloh F.2As gave a solid decade of service prior to their retirement. Although they were externally similar to the F.6, they retained the early Rolls-Royce series 211 engines, as they proved to be more fuel efficient when coupled with the aircraft's cleaner design – there were fewer scoops and vents along the fuselage of the F.2A. As a result of the aircraft's smoother exterior, the RAFG Lightnings boasted a reasonable endurance – one former F.2A pilot told me that he had flown for two hours in an aircraft unrefuelled during a high-level sortie, although he never mentioned if he was using both engines at any one time! Another plus feature of this variant was the retention of the Aden cannon, which were

Everything down, but with its airbrakes still in, 'JS' tucks in close for a pairs let down back through the 'murk' to Binbrook.

Over page:
The Lightning's low-level hunting ground was at 250 ft above the North Sea, south of Flamborough Head. Both of these aircraft served with No. 11 Sqn right to the end, before going on to serve briefly as Battle Damage Repair (BDR) airframes prior to being scrapped – only the nose section of XR754 has survived the cutter's torch.

A 'Diamond Nine' of Lightnings forms up, with each pilot trying to keep a visual check on the remaining members of the formation. This was the only occasion that the red-tailed flagship (XR770) of No. 5 Sqn flew in formation with its black-tailed counterpart (XR725) from No. 11 Sqn.

mounted on either side of the pilot, making live firing dramatic.

During the 1970s the perceived threat was for a low-level raid penetrating the West German border from the east, so most Lightning missions were consequently flown at low-level north of Gutersloh along the Osnabruck ridge. With the radar 'boot' folded away, it was a question of looking out of the cockpit to acquire the target visually, with the natural feature of the ridge to hide behind, Lightning pilots simply waited for incoming 'trade' to climb over the skyline, and thus make visual target acquisition a straightforward task. With its superb low-level handling qualities coupled to an excess thrust-to-weight ratio, the Lightning was ideally suited to this low-level visual role – one it was never initially intended to fulfil. With only a TACAN as a navigation aid (at 250 ft this was rarely used), the only way to plot your course was by map and stopwatch, although critics always said that the Lightning's fuel load was too small to allow a pilot

to fly far enough to get lost anyway!

By 1976 Nos 19 and 92 Sqns were in the process of running down. All the F.2s had been withdrawn and kept as decoys, and all aircraft were repainted in an overall olive green camouflage. This proved ideal for its low-level role, as only at high-level did the aircraft stand out. Throughout the type's association with RAF Germany, the Lightning had held 'Battle Flight' duties, which consisted of two aircraft held on permanent alert 365 days a year. Each fighter had to be airborne within five minutes of the scramble order, which was easily achievable with the Lightning. Being so close to the border, the quick reaction and superb climb performance put the aircraft in a league of its own – it was in its element. Despite its low-level role, with associated hazards, no Lightnings were lost in flying accidents whilst performing this demanding mission. Ironically, the only F.2A lost by either unit during this period was a No. 92 Sqn aircraft that entered a spin at 36,000 ft – a remarkable record over such a long period.

Travelling at around 450 knots and pulling 4 g, XR728 holds formation with the T.5 photo-chase as it pulls up into a loop.

First to retire its Lightnings was No. 19 Sqn who, in late 1976, gave up its F.2As for the Phantom FGR.2s and moved to Wildenrath, some 200 miles further west. This allowed the short-range Harrier force to move into Gutersloh, and thus be nearer to the border in case hostilities broke out. No. 92 Sqn followed suit in March 1977, the unit having taken on a number of ex-No. 19 Sqn aircraft that still had sufficient fatigue life left to last those extra few months. The unit's demise was not without incident, however, as with only a matter of weeks to go, one of its T.4s crashed following a hydraulic failure. At the time it was carrying a newly-arrived Harrier pilot on an experience flight – surely one to be forgotten. Fortunately, both pilots ejected safely.

With the rundown of so many squadrons, it was obvious that the need for a large OCU no longer existed, so Coltishall closed to Lightning operations and a new training unit was formed at Binbrook. Initially, it was planned to incorporate a small training cell under the guise of 'C' Flight within No. 11 Sqn, but it soon became obvious that an operational unit couldn't also concurrently support a 'mini OCU'. The new unit had the pick of the old OCU fleet, the size of which was shown by the fact that the RAF now had a surplus of T.5s – five were duly placed in open storage, destined never to fly again. In October 1975 the Lightning Training Flight (LTF) was formed, its role being simply to provide a sufficient number of new Lightning pilots to man the remaining squadrons at Binbrook until the aircraft was finally retired in 1988. With a squadron leader at the helm, the LTF initially had a complement of eight aircraft (four F.3s and a similar number of T.5s), although there were plenty of other aircraft held in reserve to choose from.

At its peak, there were some 80+ Lightnings on-base at Binbrook, this number comprising a few F.1A decoys, a sole T.4 'out to grass', and a large stock of F.3s, T.5s and F.6s. Despite the mass-scrapping of F.3s at Wattisham in the late 1970s, sufficient numbers of the type remained in service to see Nos 5 and 11 Sqns through until mid-1987. With its smaller wing and lighter weight, it proved an ideal mount for air combat training and aerobatics, thus preserving the life of the operational F.6s.

With the end of 'C' Flight No. 11 Sqn, the LTF became a self-contained unit and moved into the middle hangar behind Binbrook's Air Traffic Control Tower. By 1978 the Flight had taken an F.6 on strength – normally a high fatigue aircraft, as they were only used as targets. One aircraft (XR728) even bore the name 'Tiverton Target Trainer'. In later years the LTF F.6 usually had the name of the Binbrook Wing Commander Operations painted on

it, for he was directly responsible for the Flight. The aircraft, only ever flown by the staff, lacked the Aden guns and carried a forward fuel tank, which added an extra 75 gallons to its capacity. In the nose was fitted a Luneberg radar reflector, giving students those few extra miles on first detection.

No sooner had the LTF formed than it was engaged in trials to develop a suitable camouflage for the remaining fleet. Despite the fact that the RAFG Lightnings had been sprayed dark green in their later years, various schemes were trialled using some of the time-expired decoys at Binbrook. Shades of grey and green were tested before two T.5s were sprayed in a final colour scheme. One was painted grey, whilst another was resprayed in NATO green similar to that used by the F.2A force. In typical British style, a compromize was made that saw both shades chosen, and the whole fleet duly painted grey and green! Although not ideal for high level operations, the camouflage was extremely effective at low-level over the sea or land. Over the next few years squadron markings became even more inconspicuous and toned down, as the flamboyant days of the 1960s became but a distant memory for a handful of veteran Lightning pilots still flying in the frontline.

Meanwhile, the units were gearing up to an ever increasing duration at Binbrook, the stay of execution being extended as the in service date of the Tornado F.3 progressively slipped further to the right. Throughout this period the wing was responsible for holding Southern QRA, although Nos 5 and 11 Sqns never enjoyed the same level of intercept activity as the Leuchars-based FG.1s. In 1979 preparations were made at Binbrook to celebrate the Lightning's 25th year in RAF service, and during the latter part of July mass formations could be seen in the skies over Lincolnshire as the squadrons rehearsed in the weeks leading up to the 3 August event. A 22-aircraft formation had been successfully flown during the work-ups, but sadly the planned celebrations fell foul of the typically unseasonal weather that often afflicted Binbrook during the summer, and low cloud cover combined with heavy rain reduced the planned flypast from 25

The nine pilots who flew the last ever Lightning 'Diamond Nine' – from left to right, Flt Lt Paul Sutton, Sqn Ldr Paul Cooper, Flt Lt Ian Hollingworth, Wg Cdr Jake Jarron (OC of No. 11 Sqn), Grp Capt John Spencer (Binbrook Station Commander), Flt Lt Alan 'Porky' Page, Sqn Ldr John Aldington, Flt Lt John Carter and Flt Lt Chris Berners Price.

Trying to photograph nine aircraft in the same piece of sky is harder than it looks. Firstly, you need to position yourself on the correct side for the sun, taking account of any turns the formation has been briefed to make, then it's a question of patience as you wait for the split-second when all nine aircraft appear symmetrical. If the aircraft overlap then the overall balance looks wrong – it's all a question of timing.

to four, although the latter put on a spirited show. On the ground, nine aircraft were painted to represent each of the Lightning squadrons that had operated the type, and their scheduled 'Diamond Nine' formation also fell victim to the weather. In the evening over 200 guests attended a formal dinner that ended with such high spirits that the event was destined to pass into Binbrook history.

With so many aircraft visible on the base, it came as no surprise, therefore, when an announcement was made that a third squadron was to form at Binbrook to bolster the UK's air defences. Rumours ran rife as to whether No. 74 Sqn would rise phoenix-like from the ashes, although MoD officialdom would no doubt have seen the 'number plate' given to a less-deserving unit. In the end, the idea had to be abandoned due to both the costs involved and a shortage of pilots. Reforming a squadron would have also required major physical changes at Binbrook, with the LTF having to move behind the No. 11 Sqn hangars, and thus further away from the link with Air Traffic – vital on student solo sorties.

In the end the new squadron never left the in-tray, and was axed before anything happened. Nevertheless, from 1981 the LTF ran courses for former Lightning pilots to re-acquaint themselves with the aeroplane over an intensive five-day period. The courses, of which about six were run per year, came under the guise of the Lightning Augmentation Flight (LAF), and were designed for all former 'recent' Lightning pilots below the rank of wing commander. They proved to be a great success, and allowed the Lightning force to keep a reserve of ready-trained pilots in ground or staff appointments. No aircraft were allocated to the Flight on a permanent basis, although a few F.6s carried a small LAF badge in dayglo on the fin. Sadly, this scheme was short-lived, and by the mid-1980s the LAF no longer existed.

Earlier in the decade undercarriage problems had plagued the T.5 fleet, with several incidents occurring where the gear had retracted soon after landing. Indeed, the situation became so serious that some courses were run where the students flew a large part of the radar phase solo instead of in the

One of the privileges of being a fast jet pilot is the fantastic lighting conditions you experience at altitude – above 40,000 ft the sky turns a deep indigo blue. 'AD' is seen here still wearing its No. 5 Sqn colours, despite having been operated by No. 11 Sqn for well over six months by the time this shot was taken in early 1988 whilst transiting at high level from Binbrook to Warton.

'T-Bird', a staff pilot normally shadowing his pupil in a second F.3 in order to keep a check on his progress. On the general handling side, some students had to fly entire T.5 sorties with the gear locked down in order to alleviate the retraction problem. Fortunately, a cure was soon found.

The LTF finally stood down in April 1987, and sadly all five students in the last long course failed to graduate, thus proving that despite its age, the Lightning was still a challenging aircraft to fly. By this late stage in the fighter's frontline career, only a few F.3s had any useful fatigue life left in them, and the best two were duly transferred to No. 5 Sqn to fulfil the unit's display duties during its last airshow season. The rest of the LTF fleet, including the T.5s, was either scrapped or allocated to the two frontline units.

With the closure of the LTF, there was now no possibility of any last-minute reprieves for the Lightning force. A glimmer of hope had briefly existed for an extension to the life of the fleet when the Royal Saudi Air Force handed back their Lightnings in January 1986. Recovered in three waves by RAF pilots accompanied by VC10 tankers, all 22 surviving aircraft were flown back to their original birthplace at Warton – plans had also been made earlier in the decade to recover the ex-Kuwaiti Air Force machines held in open storage in the desert, but after an in-depth investigation by RAF engineers, they were found to be in too poor a condition to repair economically.

Devoid of Saudi markings, the 22 Lightnings sat in open storage at Warton, bereft of protection from the English weather for a number of years whilst attempts were made to resell them both to Austria and Nigeria – indeed, talks were fairly advanced with the latter as several senior Nigerian officers visited the LTF to see the Lightning at first hand. In the end, both countries declined the offer and the aircraft remained at Warton. The RAF were particularly interested in the two-seat T.55s, as they boasted the larger wing and bigger ventral tank of the F.6 – perfectly suited to LTF needs. However, they proved to be too different from a technical

LAST OF THE LIGHTNINGS

standpoint from the remaining RAF force, and like the F.53s, never flew again. Many of the airframes were given to museums across the UK, whilst a large cache was brought by a private collector, who had them dismantled and stored in sea containers.

Despite the constant threat of disbandment throughout the 1980s, Nos 5 and 11 Sqns continued to operate to a routine that had been established in the late 1960s, the highlights of which were standing QRA, the annual air-to-air gunnery detachment to Akrotiri and a two-week missile camp in Wales. During The Falklands War, a few aircraft began to use the overwing tanks again which had lain dormant for some time, but there was never any possibility of the aircraft being involved in the conflict due to its great distance from Binbrook – the Lightning force did, however, provide useful training for the Harrier force by acting as 'Mirage' aggressors prior to the GR.3s' deployment to the South Atlantic.

No sooner had the whole fleet been camouflaged when, in keeping with the other UK fighters then in service, trials were conducted using an overall grey scheme for the Lightning. Despite much effort going in to trialling the new camouflage, there never really was a definitive colour adopted across the fleet – as many as three different shades of grey, applied in as many different styles, were visible on Binbrook Lightnings.

In 1986, some 21 years after receiving its first interim F.6s, No. 5 Sqn had a double celebration to mark both its unbroken association with the same aircraft and its 70th anniversary. To mark the occasion some of the unit's fighters were marked up in the colours of former Lightning years, whilst the squadron flagship had its fin painted red – this was later extended to the leading edges of the wings as well. As was usual for Binbrook, the day of the celebration brought low cloud and poor visibility, but by late afternoon the cloud base had lifted sufficiently enough to launch nine aircraft and a photo chase. Sadly, the weather was too poor to perform a flypast, and the final No. 5 Sqn 'Diamond Nine' was seen only by those in the formation itself.

The last big public show of the Lightning was held on 22 August 1987, being billed as 'The Last, Last, Lightning Show'. The public were obviously aware that this was indeed the end, and turned up in their thousands – double the number originally estimated. Once again the weather proved typically bleak but, as if by some miracle, cleared sufficiently to launch the planned wing flypast. Anyone who

Transiting at low-level, a pair of Lightnings representing the last two operational squadrons to fly the ultimate British fighter head inbound to RAF Valley. The No. 5 Sqn F.3 (notice its smaller ventral tank when compared with the F.6 behind) was issued to RAF Manston as a fire training aid in late 1987, whilst the No. 11 Sqn aircraft was initially sent to RAF Leeming for use as a BDR airframe, but was rescued and taken on strength by its former operator.

For many years Lightnings fitted with overwing tanks were rarely seen at Binbrook. It was somewhat surprising then to see a number of aircraft boasting the big tanks right at the end of the aircraft's frontline career. In all six aircraft were re-modified to carry the overwing stores, these tanks greatly increasing sortie duration to the point where aerial refuelling was no longer required.

was there will never forget the sight of eleven Lightnings, led by the Station Commander Gp Capt John Spencer, taking off in typically English summer weather – low cloud, poor visibility and rain. Each Lightning took off in a stream of ten seconds from Binbrook's rain-soaked runway 21, staying low and turning right immediately after take-off. Flying low over Bully Hill, the aircraft stayed low and turned through 270° back across the field towards the crowd. As the first aircraft crossed the tarmac, others were still lifting off and tucking their wheels up in the same instant. As they approached the crowd, each Lightning, its reheats glowing like pressure cookers, soared skywards, blazing into the low stratus. The last one airborne stayed so low that vortex streamers trailing from its wingtips blew over the arrestor barrier at the far end of the runway.

While the crowd waited anxiously for their return, the Lightnings formed into a 'Diamond Nine' – so characteristic of many previous displays. As the nine-ship formation flew low over the airfield, the two solo pilots flew past from opposite directions almost on the Mach. Due to the damp weather conditions some spectacular photography was taken showing the supersonic shock waves forming over the aircraft. As the nine-ship flew past for the last time, the back four, led by Flt Lt Bob Bees, broke away to conclude the show. As each section arrived for the break to land, time was finally running out for this great fighter – within twelve months Binbrook would be closed. With only a single Lightning left to land, once again the sky filled with the roar of two Avons in full reheat as the final aircraft performed a 'burner overshoot'. To close the show, Flt Lt John Fynes performed a sparkling display in one of the last F.3s still in service.

By the end of 1987 No. 5 Sqn had disbanded and been transferred to Coningsby to re-equip with the Tornado F.3. A handful of aircraft and four of the unit's youngest pilots were moved across to No. 11 Sqn to join the 'last of the Lightnings'.

Despite the fact that the latter unit had little time left in service, it carried on with its normal commitments right up until the end of April 1988 –

No. 11 Sqn put up its final 'Diamond Nine' on the 29th of that month, before promptly standing down. For the next two months the remaining pilots were kept busy trying to use up the fatigue life left on all the airframes, as well as delivering Lightnings to various stations across the UK. The distinction of flying the last true RAF flight fell to Sqn Ldrs John Aldington and Paul Cooper when they delivered two F.6s to a private buyer at Cranfield on 30 June 1988. This final flight represented the end of an era for the RAF, and although 1988 should have seen the end of Lightning operations, period, once again fate saved the day.

In late 1987 No. 5 Sqn had flown an aircraft in the overwing tank fit, duly providing a sight that had not been seen for a number of years. The purpose of these sorties was to return several aircraft back to British Aerospace Warton as targets for the Tornado F.3 radar programme. Ultimately, six aircraft were re-modified to carry the big tanks, although only four were returned to the company. With so many surplus Phantom FG.1s/FGR.2s around it seemed an odd choice to use the tired Lightnings for this role, but a rumour circulated at the time stating that it would have been bad for the company's image to be seen operating American aircraft, probably stands true. In the end these aircraft soldiered on until 1993, when the final flight was performed in January of that year – nearly 40 years after the first prototype had initially flown. The legend of the Lightning has since been kept alive by a handful of individuals who have exhibited examples in museums across Britain. With some retained in airworthy condition, it is hoped that one day the sky will again be filled with the sight and sound of Britain's best-loved jet-powered fighter.

CHAPTER 2

OCU

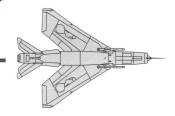

In 1986 the choices of posting available to a pilot who had just successfully completed the Tactical Weapons Unit (TWU) course were somewhat greater than they are today. You were either assessed as suitable single-seat or multi-crew, before being further sub-divided into either air defence or ground attack, with the Buccaneer falling between the two, but leaning more towards ground attack. The latter comprised either the Jaguar or Harrier for single-seat capable students, or the Tornado GR.1. For air defenders, the options available were either the two-seat Phantom FG.1/FGR.2 or the mighty Lightning.

Despite the latter's advancing age, only the cream of the TWU graduates were posted onto the 'beast' because of its exceptionally high cockpit work load. I had spent the early 1980s navigating Phantom FGR.2s in RAFG, so there was no way I wanted to go back to the front seat of an aircraft that I'd just left. There was only one choice – the Lightning – unquestionably the ultimate British-built fighter.

Having spent my youth growing up around the Lightning at various East Anglian fighter bases, I used to dream that one day I'd manage a trip in one just as a passenger – to pilot one was pure fantasy.

High in the upper atmosphere, F.3 'DA' of the LTF displays its clean lines – this aircraft was one of a pair of F.3s taken on strength by No. 5 Sqn following the closure of the LTF specifically for display work during the Lightning's final airshow season.

From this angle the F.6 looked less than glamorous, the large underbelly tank and cranked wings being less refined than the lithe F.3.

Everything about the aircraft captured me. I just had to fly it. Having begged for the chance to cross-train from navigator to pilot in 1984, it had finally taken me two-and-a-half years to reach the end of the TWU course until the inevitable day of posting arrived.

Throughout the three months at Brawdy I knew that every sortie counted towards your ultimate aircraft choice. In particular, those with an air-to-air flavour like the ciné weave – a tracking exercise where you had to keep your gunsight fixed on the lead Hawk as he gyrated around the sky at 4g. It initially seemed an impossible task, with the crude comment of 'trying to stuff spaghetti up a wild cat's backside' being perhaps the best analogy I've yet heard to describe this mission. Then came the air combat phase, where you had to try and 'shoot down' an instructor who knew your every move, and more besides. Lastly came the air-to-air gunnery, where the scores were literally 'on the door'.

Being proficient at the air defence exercises wasn't good enough to get you a fighter posting, however, as you had to show an above average ability in instrument flying, plus complete the low-level simulated attack phase satisfactorily. Your ability to handle both these areas adequately indicated to the instructors just how much spare capacity you had to deal with things when they didn't go exactly to plan. These sorties also allowed the TWU staff to gauge how you would cope in a high work load environment.

Traditionally, each pilot is told his posting in a less than orthodox manner. My unit's (No. 234 Sqn) tradition was to stick the name of your aircraft type on the base of a glass-bottomed beer tankard, the contents of which had to be 'drunk in one' so as to reveal the good or bad news. Posting time came, and I can recall apprehensively downing my pint until I could read the word 'LIGHTNING' written on the bottom of the glass – the dream had started. Now at last I had a chance to join the elite force – the rest of my course were sent to the Harrier GR.3 or Phantom FGR.2 communities.

Within a week I'd packed my bags and departed the west Welsh coast bound for RAF North Luffenham, home of the air force's Aviation

Medicine Department. Here, I met my other Lightning course colleague, a former Canberra pilot who was attempting a fast jet cross over. Before I'd even started at Binbrook, I could already sense how difficult it would be to fit into the cockpit as I was constantly being measured and weighed to check that my arms weren't too long or my legs too short. Each type of aircraft cockpit is different, with some, like the Victor and Buccaneer, having restrictions placed on crew height and leg length. The Lightning was a typically British fighter, being 'a bit tight around the shoulders', but despite my 6 ft 2 ins frame, I still seemed to fit into the aircraft. Minute examinations of ears and sinuses were also made, as it was assumed that most of our flying life would be spent at an altitude of around 50,000 ft at speeds approaching Mach 2.0 – a hangover from the Lightning high altitude interception tasking of the 1960s, no doubt. Between fittings for survival equipment, I sat in the coffee bar talking to ex-Lightning pilot Grp Capt Harry Drew, who had also flown the USAF's U-2 on an exchange posting. He told me at great length how lucky we were, and gave us a few tips on how to save fuel by constantly

checking the engine nozzle positions – advice that stuck with me throughout my short sojourn on the Lightning. Having been told that we were the last two students destined for the LTF, we left Luffenham in trepidation, hoping that no one would close the Flight early and redirect us to the 'massed rank and file' of the Phantom II OCU.

Driving up the hill to RAF Binbrook brought back childhood memories of snow, howling gales and frequent rain, not to mention fog – all of which was soon to become a way of life again. If you were ever lucky enough to have visited the LTF crew room you would surely recall one of the most wonderful pieces of aviation wall art to grace an RAF fighter station. Painted in the late 1970s (if memory serves me, by Vaughn Radford, a founder member of No. 74 Sqn), the wall-length mural depicted an early flying machine much modified to incorporate all the major parts of a two-seat Lightning – it was a real work of art.

Having just graduated as a steely-eyed fighter pilot from the TWU, I was made to feel more than a little humble thanks to the proliferation of 1,000-hour Lightning patches that adorned the flying suits

The number of 'perfect' days for photography in the UK are few and far between. This shot was taken on such occasion in winter when the sun shone and the sky was filled with puffy white cumulus clouds. XS898 'BD' sits on the Valley ramp, armed with live Red Top missiles.

Come rain or shine, life went on at Binbrook. Justifiably known as the RAF's last true 'fightertown', the Lincolnshire station always exuded a positive atmosphere, even when its final days were numbered. When the station was holding QRA duties the runway had to remain clear at all times.

of the LTF instructors. The flying side of the RAF provides one of life's great levellers, where the saying 'you're only as good as your last trip' is never more true. All the LTF pilots had completed one tour with either of the resident Binbrook units or, exceptionally, a tour on earlier mark Lightnings in the pre-Binbrook days – by 1986 the number of current pilots who had flown the Lightning operationally in Germany, Cyprus or Singapore was dwindling fast. All the staff were either IWIs (Intercept Weapons Instructors), Qualified Flying Instructors (QFIs) or Tactics Instructors (TIs).

Having had the obligatory arrival brief from the boss of the LTF, it was outside for the equally obligatory course photo. This was taken with the LTF flagship – a high-fatigue F.6 target aircraft – providing the backdrop. As mentioned earlier in this

volume, LTF F.6s were fitted with an extra fuel tank in place of the gun pack for increased endurance when operating as an airborne target for the unit's T.5s and F.3s.

Walking back through the wartime hangars towards the simulator, I quickly gauged just how complex an aircraft the Lightning was, as the entire floor-space was covered by airframes in various states of maintenance. Next to each skeletal shell lay a pile of parts that made you wonder if they would all go back together again – evidently this was no Hawk. The ground school was conducted just behind the LTF hangar, and was a fairly civilized two-week affair. The first week was filled with aircraft systems' lectures, notably focusing on the airframe engines, electrics, fuel and hydraulics.

In order to avoid the student being saturated with

Ground crews would work long and hard to keep the airfield open throughout winter, despite frequent snow falls. XS922 was despatched to Wattisham for BDR, where its mortal remains were finally scrapped in 1992.

facts right from the start of the course, radar and weapons systems were covered once the flying had commenced. The second week saw us thrown into the simulator for emergency drills and general handling exercises. Fortunately, use of the 'four-inch torture tube' (situated in the right-hand corner of the cockpit, and more commonly known as the AI.23 radar) was saved until after the basic conversion phase had been completed. The end of a week's basic simulator flying left me feeling that the next six months were not going to be easy. During the second week I took every opportunity to walk up to the LTF hangar and sit in a T.5, where I vainly tried to learn the left to right cockpit checks. The two-seater was, of course, very different from the simulator, which reproduced the F.3/F.6 cockpit.

With ground school completed, it was off to the LTF to begin the CONVEX (Conversion Exercises)

phase, which normally comprised five dual sorties, followed by a solo. Prior to commencing the assessed flying, a passenger flight was given to pupils as an incentive if time allowed. This was usually performed in a T.5 that required an air test following the completion of rectification work. After the first solo there was then a mixture of dual and solo sorties expanding the handling envelope of the aircraft. Initially, the emphasis was placed on circuit flying for the first ten sorties, followed by a concentrated period of instrument flying which culminated in the Instrument Rating Test (IRT). At this stage the simulator was invaluable as it was able to faithfully reproduce the aircraft under instrument flying conditions. Due to the T.5's minimal fuel reserves, it wasn't possible to accomplish the whole IRT in one sortie, so an in-cockpit turn around was performed, and the two sorties flown back-to-back –

The author right, and Flt Lt Martin Durham, the two students on No. 73 Lightning course. This should have been the last course, however two more followed afterwards, though like my fellow course pilot, they all failed to make the grade.

An in-cockpit view of the T.5 trainer. Dominating the instrument panel is the artificial horizon indicator, which worked very reliably on a roller blind system.

unless, of course, you were able to find a tanker. The test was followed by a period of close and tactical formation flying, which came as a welcome break after having had your eyes glued to the dials for two weeks. At the end of the formation flying phase a handling check was performed, prior to the start of the radar phase. If you were already having difficulty getting to grips with the Lightning at this early stage in the course, then there was little hope for you with the addition of radar handling to the syllabus.

The two-seat T.5 had an awkward cockpit both in terms of its size and instrument layout – indeed, it would probably be labelled today as 'unacceptable', or an ergonomic disaster. All the main flight instruments were grouped in the centre of the cockpit, which gave an instant parallax problem due to the side-by-side seating arrangement. Both cockpit walls came fitted with independent throttle quadrants and a radar hand controller, the student normally manipulating these from the left hand seat (just as in a conventional single-seater), with the staff pilot occupying the right. Despite its inability to carry guns, the trainer was nevertheless fitted with a gunsight on the left-hand side. Engine gauges were

placed on the left side, whilst the less important navigation and lighting controls were placed on the right.

My first impression of the T.5 – or 'Tub', as it was affectionately known – was somewhat off-putting. It felt like an enormous feline beast waiting to pounce on the unwary. There was no comparison between it and the diminutive Hawk which I had flown just two weeks before. The Lightning's cockpit was some ten feet off the ground, and could only be entered using the awkward access ladder which threaded its way between the fuselage and the wing-mounted refuelling probe – entry via the right-hand side was somewhat easier thanks to the absence of the lance-like refuelling probe. You had to be a contortionist to climb the ladder in full flying kit whilst going up and under the probe in order to gain access to the cockpit. At first strapping in was a lengthy and laborious procedure, having come from the Hawk which had the latest Mk 10 seat with its simple lap and shoulder strap assembly. By contrast, the Lightning had all manner of straps, buckles and quick release boxes, all of which had to be arranged in an eye-pleasing manner.

Prior to each sortie commencing, all pilots passed

Whilst taking part in NATO *Exercise Mallet Blow 87*, I was unexpectedly joined on CAP by the No. 5 Sqn T.5. Flown by Mike Chatterton and Alf Moir, they quickly announced over the intercom that their radar was unserviceable and therefore latched onto my wing for eventual guidance back to Binbrook. However, with the T.5's limited fuel reserves, my first task was to find them a tanker, which in the carefree days of the late 1980s was not a problem.

My 'mentor' and 'minder' when I first arrived on No. 11 Sqn was the moustachioed Steve Hunt, seen here in his 'office'.

Viewed from above XV328 was the penultimate Lightning for the RAF

line, situated between the two operational squadrons on the large concrete apron. In winter, performing this normally mundane chore could in itself be a precarious exercise, as the 'pan' was often awash with spilled and leaking jet fuel. The flight line was a sight now rarely seen on frontline bases within the RAF due to the advent of Hardened Aircraft Shelters (HASs). With up to 30 Lightnings aligned in symmetrical fashion, it made for an impressive sight.

Arriving at your assigned Lightning, your first task was to make sure the aeroplane was safe then perform the walkaround check in customary left to right fashion. As with all service aircraft, each pilot first checked that there was a fire extinguisher available, the chocks were in place and that nothing obvious was amiss. Following you around the aircraft, the ground crew would remove all intake blanks and ground locks. Starting at the front, a quick push on the nose wheel doors ensured that they were free, before you moved onto the radar bullet. Here, the pilot would look for burn holes caused by radar emissions, as well as generally checking the condition of the fibre-glass structure itself. Mounted above the radome was the standby pitot tube, which was checked for blockages, followed by a glance down the intake for foreign object damage before moving onto the right side of the fuselage. Looking under the ventral and wing areas, you would check the surfaces for fuel leaks, or

through the LTF line hut to read and sign their aircraft's individual RAF Form 700. Basically like a car service manual, it logged details of all rectification work carried out and any minor faults carried. Having signed for the aircraft, it was then just a matter of a short walk out to the LTF flight

Sqn Ldr John 'B J' Aldington runs through his pre-start checks whilst strapping into XR754 'BC'. This aircraft was originally completed in 1965 as an 'interim' F.6, before being upgraded at Warton to full spec two years later. It ended its days at Honnington as a ground decoy, with only the nose section surviving after it was scrapped in 1992.

at least for leaks that were from the right place – Lightnings were notorious for leaking, but as long as the fluid was dripping from the appropriate drain holes it was acceptable. The tyres came under the spotlight next, and these had to be closely inspected especially on a windy day, when they could get worn out on a single take-off and landing. With Binbrook's runway being set at 030/210°, easterly winds often made for some fairly sporting crosswinds, so if the pilot expressed any doubts concerning the state of his tyres, the engineers would change the wheel in a matter of minutes. Around the back of the aircraft on the right-hand side were five accumulator gauges, all of which had to be displaying readings within the limits laid down in the pilot's check list. By the time I arrived on the Lightning force some of the aircraft had been repainted several times and these gauges were nearly impossible to read, often being almost obliterated by paint.

Looking into the two tail pipes, you checked for any signs of molten metal deposits, which were a sure sign of impending engine failure. Wrapped around the two jet pipes was the cable for the brake parachute, stored in a figure of eight fashion and secured with clips and a bolt at the top of the upper loop – how this stayed in at 650 knots I still don't know. On several occasions the reheat burnt away parts of the cable, and recoveries were made with cable streaming from the back end. On the left side of the rear fuselage another important check that had to be diligently carried out focused on contents of the fire extinguisher, the presence of positive indicators denoting that the bottle contents had not been discharged. Before climbing the ladder, the pilot gave the weapons pack a final look over to ensure that the missiles carried were undamaged. Then, as a final check at the top of the ladder, a glance over the wing upper surface to have a final look for fuel venting.

Having strapped in and checked that all the main instruments were switched off, the aircraft's battery was then selected to 'on' and the seat raised or lowered to check its charge. If all was operating as advertised, a quick signal to the ground crew saw the external power connected to provide AC and DC power to the aircraft. As with so many things associated with the Lightning, even the type of ground crew that serviced the aircraft no longer exists. They were known as flight line mechanics, or 'Flems' for short, and they would work on the Lightnings outside in all weathers, doing minor rectification and post-flight servicing, as well as performing other minor 'mechanical miracles'. Moving from left to right, you completed the internal pre-start checks – which normally took a good ten minutes on the first few sorties, but after a few months could be completed in a matter of seconds. Eventually, your eyes became so accustomed to how the cockpit should be set up prior to engine start that any switch that was out of place was instantly spotted. Towards the end of their lives all Lightning cockpits had a decidedly well-worn and lived in appearance. Any paint that had originally been applied to the various switches had long since disappeared, and they all bore a shiny, well-worn, look after years of hard use.

Prior to engine start, a radio call was made to Binbrook tower to check that the radio was serviceable – this also served the dual purpose of ensuring that contact could be made with the fire section should the aircraft catch fire when started up. Having checked that the throttles had full and free movement, you gave the ground crewman the start signal with your left hand – a circling motion with one index finger extended. It was important that he acknowledged this, and in turn gave you clearance to start the number one engine as hot gases were expelled from beneath the aircraft during the ignition sequence, and anyone standing nearby could have been badly burnt. Having had your 'wind up' signal returned, you then moved the throttle on the number one engine forward in order to open the HP (High Pressure) cock and pull up the rapid start gang bar, whilst making sure that the fuel

pumps came on line. Then, like a scene from a Jules Verne film, you pressed the start button and awaited the unknown. Instantly, a loud hissing noise, followed by an explosion, occurred behind you as half a gallon of Avpin (Iso-propyl-nitrate) ignited inside its combustion chamber to propel the number one Avon engine into life. Avpin is a highly dangerous 'mono' combustible fuel which can burn without oxygen, and is highly flammable. Many Lightnings bore stains where the fuselage met the spine, spilt Avpin having removed all the paint down to the bare metal.

The experience of starting an Avon engine is not easily forgotten, and for the novice there were many traps to avoid, not least of which was failing to maintain a watchful eye on the wind direction. As the Avpin combusted it gave off acrid fumes which could flow straight back into the cockpit area if the wind was blowing in the wrong direction, resulting in your eyes streaming and a burning sensation in your throat. Wiping watery tears from your vision, an eagle eye had to be kept on the JPT (Jet Pipe Temperature) gauge as the temperature rise would show how the start was progressing. The back end quickly reached 800°C, and with the wind behind on a hot summer's day, an 'over temp' was very likely. As the RPM rose, you checked that the fire lights were out and all the pressures – oil, hydraulics and accumulators – were rising. The throttle was then set to the incredibly slow idle speed of 34 per cent. With the number one engine running, you could either bring the power up and start the number two from the number one, or leave the external power connected.

The Lightning was infamous for not starting, especially during the winter months or on damp and foggy days. On the Binbrook flight line, it was not an uncommon sight to see ground crew clambering up onto the spine of a Lightning and set about the starter unit with a hammer, or having to resort to pouring hot water through the pipes in order to coax them to life freeing stuck air valves. Once, during an overseas deployment, an aircraft refused to start due to a stuck air valve being the cause. With no compressed air available, an alternative

With the sun glistening off its slab-sided fuselage, XR769 awaits its pilot prior to performing a night mission. Not long after this photograph was taken, the aircraft went to a watery grave after its pilot was forced to eject following an inflight fire.

Flt Lt Alan Page is seen in the cockpit of an F.6 just prior to performing the last public display of a Lightning. The people of North Coates were treated to a spirited final demonstration of the aircraft's might by this long time pilot.

60

solution had to be found, so after a little head scratching, a spare wheel was brought over and a length of pipe attached to the high-pressure tyre valve. The makeshift compressor quickly blew open the stuck valve.

Another big draw back of the Avpin starting system was that the reservoir only held six gallons of liquid. This allowed just one start, plus a reserve for a further two starts should the aircraft land away at another base. Avpin levels could be increased, however, by adopting a 'Hot Top-Up' procedure – not officially permitted – which saw the tank quickly refilled after the engines had started. Needless to say, the employment of an explosive system to start the Lightning's engines resulted in a number accidents occurring over its many years in service. Due to the risks involved with Avpin, there were strict rules to be adhered to should an engine fail to start after pressing the starter button. Various types of failures had differing remedies, but it was obviously unwise to persist in trying to start the engine if little was happening. This happened to F.6 XS923 when the pilot tried on several occasions to start the engines but each time met with no success. Unbeknown to

him, each attempt put more Avpin into the combustion chamber until the inevitable reaction occurred – the resulting explosion blew the starter unit horizontally through the fuselage beneath his feet and out of the Lightning via the radome. Despite its volatile nature, the start system was relatively simple to operate and rapid in its execution – indeed, on a scramble start you could have started both engines simultaneously, although regulations did not permit this.

The start sequence for the number two engine was identical, but before external power was pulled away the throttle was opened up to 65 per cent, or fast idle, thus keeping the aircraft's air turbine generator on line. With both engines now running, relatively few checks were required prior to taxying, other than quickly confirming that the ejector seat pins were out and your elbows were in when the time came to close the canopy. With the shutting of the latter, any previous misconceptions you had about the cockpit being roomy were now quickly dispelled. Once the hood was down and locked, you felt like a mouse trapped in a cage, surrounded by iron work. A final check was now made on the

'Airborne'. Without a doubt the Lightning was the 'king of the roller-skate take-off'. With the 'burners in and the gear up, the aircraft simply hugged the runway until the boundary fence appeared. However, a few over-enthusiastic pilots were forced to leave the aircraft during its three decades of service courtesy of 'Mr Martin-Baker' because of rather overzealous departures.

From low-level to high
altitude, the Lightning was
always as steady as a rock.

Spurn Point was a familiar
landmark to all pilots who
operated from Binbrook, as it
stood out from the air and was
easy to find on radar. When
performing a visual recovery to
base it was the best sight
around, as everyone knew that
if you held a heading of 220°
from here, within three
minutes you'd be in the
Binbrook overhead.

brake pressure, before a quick flick of the taxi light to indicate ready to taxi and you release the parking brake, ingeniously located on the control column. With the parking brake off, and the engines set at idle/fast idle, the aircraft quickly pounced forward. Squeezing the brake lever on the stick, the 'Tub' would nod down to show that both brakes were working. A small kick of the right foot and a deft squeeze of the brake lever would see the nose inch around with plenty of excess power to taxi, even at idle. The aeroplane was gloriously overpowered even on the ground 30 years after its maiden flight.

Taxying soon became second nature after a few sorties, and the only criticism was that one hand had to stay on the control column at all times in order to operate the brakes. This usually wasn't a great problem, however, as it was virtually impossible to retrieve anything from your leg pockets as they were both firmly squeezed into the narrow cockpit foot wells. In the two-seater you needed to keep your head moving at all times in order to keep a look out for other aircraft, or vehicles, on the ground. Even with the canopy down, the interior noise level was quite high, with the aeroplane giving the impression of being alive, humming and vibrating with life. Trying to taxy the Lightning whilst simultaneously running through the pre-take-off checks proved to be a bit of a handful at first, but as with everything, practice soon made perfect. If all other systems subsequently failed on take off, the following four last-minute line up checks would at least allow you to get airborne safely – Controls, check that they were full and free; Captions, that they were all out; Pins, that you had four stowed and the seat was live; and finally, Canopy, down and locked.

Having obtained take-off clearance, lining up on the centreline of the runway was not as easy as it looked, with its ultra thin high-pressure tyres, the Lightning would skid and slide very easily on wet, or slippery, concrete, and particularly on the white-painted 'piano keys' at the runway threshold. Although the nose wheel was self-centring on

I've heard this lighting phenomena described as 'Holy Light' – impudent 'fingers' of light stabbing at the ground below. Caught in the sun's rays is the No. 11 Sqn T.5, returning from an exercise held at Rheims, in France.

Right to the end the Warton F.6 retained its natural metal scheme, having avoided the paint shop for almost a quarter of a century. XP693 is seen here just seconds away from touchdown on Valley's long runway. As a general rule, 'touch and goes' were not performed by the Lightning due to the excessive wear they inflicted on the thin, high-pressure, tyres.

retraction, it wasn't whilst on the ground. You therefore had to be quite sure you were aligned straight down the runway. If not, when you released the brakes you careered off at an angle, with disastrous consequences on a pairs take-off. Whilst squeezing the brakes, the throttles were slowly advanced to a matched position of 92 per cent, whilst all the while you kept a watchful eye on both the JPTs and the warning captions. Satisfied with proceedings, the brakes were now released and the throttles pushed smoothly forward to full dry power, resulting in the RPM winding up to 103 per cent and the JPT staying around 795°C. Following a quick check of the nozzle indicators, a glance at the ASI (Air Speed Indicator) would show a reading of 100 knots, this figure being cross-checked with the standby ASI. The slight bump of the Lightning crossing the arrestor cable was another cross-check to ensure that things were going as normal. On a pilot's early sorties, his mind was still probably thinking about waving away external power back on the flight line as the aircraft passed through the 135-knot mark, signalling that it was time to rotate – stick back and the nose wheel lifted off, stick back and the Lightning was airborne at 155 knots.

The LTF had an unofficial record for the student ground speed record which stood near the 200-knot mark – the time when the student had caught up with the aeroplane sufficiently to get airborne.

At 155 knots the 'Tub' was airborne, but it still felt slightly tail heavy as it only required dry power for take-off. A 'burner take off was a different story entirely, however. With its fairly high nose-up attitude, care was needed not to scrape the Lightning's tail on rotation, and the gear was left a short pause before retraction. Airborne with a positive rate of climb, the gear was selected up followed by the customary 'clunk' and spin of the nosewheel. A cursory check of the undercarriage retraction lights showed three greens change to three reds, prior to going out, thus indicating that the gear was up and the doors were locked.

On your first trip your brain was still in the crew room as the speed quickly reached 450 knots, signalling time to either commence climbing or

Staying in close formation on your leader's wing requires 100 per cent concentration – more so in cloud. Flown by the Binbrook Station Commander Grp Capt John Spencer, 'JS' stays 'welded' to the leader's wing down to 200 ft – the operating minimum. As this height is reached, the leader lines up on his side of the runway, whilst the number two divides his attention between looking forward and staying in formation. Only when he is happy does he commit to landing on his side of the runway.

throttle back. It was at this stage in the sortie that it became apparent that with the nose 10° to 15° above the horizon, the aircraft was motoring – even in cold power. A standard climb out from Binbrook was a left-hand turn after take-off onto a heading of 040° through Airway Blue 1 up to 25,000 ft. You would usually achieve this height over Spurn Point, some 15 miles north of the airfield, immediately after which you carried out a fuel check. Already the small underbelly ventral tank would be empty, leaving only wing and flap fuel to complete the sortie. On the initial trip just a few turns were performed to expose you to the Lightning's basic handling characteristics, and thus illustrate just how docile the aircraft was, and how much buffet occurred at low speed. There is no marked stall on a swept-wing aircraft – rather indications that needed to be recognized like the nose attitude being very high, the stick a long way back into the pit of the stomach and heavy buffet. As power was never a problem in the Lightning, stall situations could usually be recovered with the application of full power.

With the fuel disappearing fast, attention now turned to running through a simulated downwind circuit leg at height to give the student a foretaste of what lay ahead on future flights. Pulling back on the power, the speed soon decayed through 250 knots, after which the undercarriage was selected 'down', the fuel checked, flaps selected 'down', harness tight and locked and a last check to ensure that you have three greens and the landing gear toggle was secured in the locked position. Tipping into the final turn onto an imaginary runway, the Lightning required a bit of pull on the stick and a boot of rudder to get it going 'round the corner' with its speed reducing through 200 knots. Going back 'head in' the cockpit, the pilot would quickly check the instruments for speed, angle of bank and rate of descent. Holding the former at 190 knots (not difficult with small stabs of power), the pilot looked to roll out onto the runway heading at 175 knots, selecting an aiming point near the 'piano keys'. He would then check that his touchdown point stayed firmly fixed in the same place in the windscreen, thus ensuring that the Lightning wasn't climbing or descending on the approach path. Satisfied of his progress, the pilot then 'popped' the airbrakes out, which allowed a higher throttle setting to be selected, and therefore achieve a more immediate response from the engines. These devices also provided instantaneous extra thrust when selected in should it appear that you were likely to land short.

Still holding your imaginary runway on the nose, you would aim to cross the threshold at 170 knots and touch down 'on the numbers' at 165. Selecting airbrakes in and gear and flaps up, you would open the throttles once again and climb away, prior to returning to base for a PAR (Precision Approach Radar) recovery. This made use of the base radar to guide you in on a precision approach, rather than by the much quicker visual recovery. The former gave the student a little more breathing space before attempting a visual run in and break. Nevertheless, on the initial conversion sorties a straightforward GCA (Ground-Controlled Approach) would still test a pupil to the limits of his capacity. Going 'head in' for the descent, the throttles were set to idle/idle and the cockpit demist turned on. At this point in proceedings it was crucial to remember to bring one engine back to fast idle to avoid the generator dropping off line. On later sorties the radar would be used to 'paint' the coast, revealing land marks at Spurn Point, as well as the Grimsby docks. As a Lightning student, you placed total trust in Binbrook Air Traffic to bring you home, all the time keeping up a constant scan on the speed, altitude and the fuel gauge. Having the aeroplane perfectly trimmed was the secret to instrument flying, as once this had been done, it tended not to wander.

Having reached your pre-determined decision height of 400 ft, you would look up from the instruments to get visual on the runway and overshoot. Unlike most other fighters, with the Lightning you applied full power and retracted the airbrakes, but crucially left the flaps and undercarriage in the 'down' position, thus minimizing fatigue damage on the latter. At 500 ft you throttled back to stop the speed racing away, and began a gentle climbing turn, with 60° of bank, commenced to the right on runway 21. The aim was now to be at 1,000 ft down wind with all the checks complete, dashing along at 200 knots. The gear and

flaps remained down, a quick check to see that the parking brake was off and that the fuel remaining was sufficient to overshoot.

On a right-hand circuit, sitting in the left seat, you were now blind to the runway, which lay off to your right side. Resorting to instruments, you flew the runway reciprocal heading whilst trying desperately to remember the last wind direction air traffic gave you to offset for drift. Keeping the height at 1,000 ft, the speed would now come back to 190 knots for the final turn, which you rolled into it calling 'Finals. Three greens', whilst pulling back firmly on the stick and kicking in a bit of rudder to keep the aircraft going round the turn – the feature of a swept-wing fighter. As the speed decayed you had to constantly trim back. The trimmer was inexorably slow on the aircraft, and it soon became clear to me why so many Lightning pilots had a worn patch on their right-hand glove thumb – the trimmer was working as fast as the pilot at this point in the approach to landing. Inside the cockpit, you pulled to the light buffet and felt the characteristic 'burble' it produced. Despite the buffet, you were still a

With the weak winter sunlight glistening off its nose, XR713 comes to a halt, brake parachute billowing. The faint spray of water kicked up by the tyres denotes the passing of a recent rain shower. This F.3 was delivered to Leuchars for BDR training in March 1987, but has since been rescued by ex-Lightning operators No. 111 Sqn, with whom it served between 1965 and 1971.

comfortable margin away from stalling the Lightning, and if things got worse a quick jab on the throttles would soon get you back on the right side of the 'drag curve'. Halfway around finals the air brakes were 'popped' so as to allow higher power setting to be chosen than was technically necessary. As you approached the runway centreline, your thumb was still trimming back to give the aeroplane its distinctive stalky, nose up, attitude on finals.

Things were happening very fast now as you allowed the speed to bleed off to 175 knots, whilst all the while looking to 'cross the fence' at 165, and thus arrive 'on the numbers' (and no where else) at 160. If you made a mistake and the touchdown looked likely to be well past the threshold, the only option was to overshoot – under no circumstances were you permitted to achieve the touchdown point by significantly reducing the power, as almost one-third of the aircraft's lift came from the vertical component of thrust in the final approach phase. The final check performed immediately prior to committing to landing was to confirm that the gear

and flaps were indeed down. With this satisfactorily completed, you now divided your attention between speed and runway.

Just as you felt you were six inches from the 'deck', it was airbrakes in, power up and into the overshoot – 'touch and goes', or 'rollers', were rarely tried as they wore out the tyres too quickly. Climbing away it was straight into another circuit for perhaps a flapless approach this time round, which would see you extended slightly, with the addition of an extra ten knots of speed – care had to be taken not to scrape the tail with the higher nose attitude. Single-engine circuits were little different from the norm thanks to the huge excess of available thrust. To prepare the student for a bad weather recovery, a low-level circuit was flown with a downwind leg halved from 1,000 to just 500 ft and the final turn extended until the aircraft intersected the normal angle of descent on approach. With the fuel burning away at an outrageous rate, it was now time to land.

Approaching for the final time, you would call

Air Traffic to inform them that you were 'Precautionary', thus letting them know that should you lose the brake 'chute following its deployment on touchdown you would be nevertheless staying on the ground due to the lack of remaining fuel aboard the Lightning. Whilst rolling out on finals, you made doubly sure that your touchdown point was going to be 'on the numbers' by pegging your speed at between 160 to 175 knots. If you landed past the 'numbers' even ten knots faster than the recommended figure, there was a good chance that you would end up in the barrier due to the relatively poor performance of the aircraft's brakes. Once 'over the fence', you planted the Lightning firmly on the concrete, whilst simultaneously pulling the 'chute handle and retarding both throttles to idle. One of the few advantages of the T.5 from the instructor's point of view was the positioning of the

throttle quadrant on the right cockpit wall. On my early sorties I always thought that my instructor was totally at ease with my flying as he would nonchalantly rest his right arm on the cockpit wall. I later learned that he had his hand firmly wedged against the back of the throttles so should you have decided to cut the power early, a physical human 'backstop' would prevent it – self-preservation was the order of the day on the LTF.

Waiting for the characteristic tug of the drag 'chute, you were now firmly committed to staying on *terra firma* come what may. As with the F.3, the T.5 had no arrestor hook, so the only other option available to you in an emergency once you had landed was the barrier. As the 'chute billowed out, the nose would lift slightly, but a generous squeeze on the brake soon put the weight firmly back down on the wheels. Having selected idle/idle, the RPM

With the 'last of the Lightnings' lined up with guardsman-like precision, LTF T.5 XS458 returns to dispersal, mission accomplished.

Seemingly on top of the world, the pilot of XP741 uses full top rudder and has the stick hard over as he holds a knife-edge position for the benefit of the author's camera.

Facing page:
Radar boot extended, the author searches for the elusive 'blip' during a high-level intercept flown in his F.6.

dropped on both engines, which caused the air turbine generator to 'drop off line', and thus activate the 'cockpit clangers' – audio attention getters, with all the associated lights flashing.

Unquestionably the trickiest landings to perform in a Lightning were those subjected to a strong crosswind on a wet runway. In these conditions the aircraft's slab-sided fuselage and large fin area made the Lightning a real handful. Thin tyres and the weather-cocking effect of the brake parachute further complicated matters – pilots would often appear in the crew room ashen faced after a night landing on a wet and windy runway. On occasions you needed both hands on the stick, with full in to wind aileron and boot-fulls of rudder to keep the aircraft from leaving the runway.

With an average dual sortie being just 30 to 35 minutes long, the learning curve was, by necessity, very steep in order to allow a student to reach the required standard that would see him go solo after just five sorties. This could mean as little as two-and-a-half hours of total dual flying prior to your

first solo sortie – you were usually cleared to go up solo as long as your landings were shown to be safe. Having had a taste of operating the Lightning in the circuit, the second sortie on the LTF syllabus was slightly less demanding as it served as an introduction to aerobatics. If you thought that the fuel consumption was high before, then this trip served as a real eye-opener as the sortie length was just 20 to 25 minutes long! Using a base height of 10,000 ft, a loop was commenced at 450 knots in full cold power. As the speed decayed, it was easy to feel the buffet as the aircraft went over the top. On the way down speed built up quickly, but by increasing the g, and therefore buffet, it was fairly easy to control. At the end of the sortie another instrument approach was usually performed, this time making use of the ILS (Instrument Landing System) – a pilot-interpreted instrument that requires no assistance from Air Traffic, except for a safety surveillance as the aircraft descends towards the runway.

The remaining three dual sorties usually

comprised more circuit work or focused on other weak areas, but they included a practice 'crash' diversion to another airfield. Due to its limited fuel supply, the Lightning was normally flown to lower fuel reserves than other frontline aircraft, so a real diversion away from Binbrook was always treated as an emergency, for on arrival at the nominated diversion airfield, the aeroplane would be literally 'flying on the fumes'.

An immediate heading was taken for the diversion field and a climb initiated on two engines. Once level at the optimum cruise height, the aircraft was flown on the number two engine, with the number one at idle. Then all fuel was transferred to the number one engine. Power would then be brought up on the number one and the number two shut down. This left you flying on the number one engine with the number two shut down. This procedure was often the downfall of students, who got confused and tried to transfer the wrong way, and

ended up shutting down the engine with all the available fuel to it. Of course the ever watchful LTF instructor intervened before things got out of hand. Binbrook diversions were to either Waddington, Coningsby or Finningley.

The aircraft had a limitation that to select an ILS frequency it had to be pre-set into the selector box by the use of different crystals. This rather antiquated system meant that only 12 different beacons could be used, but this restriction rarely posed many problems to a Lightning pilot, as there were never more than a dozen airfields close enough for the aircraft to reach on diversion in any case!

Having attained the required standard to be declared 'Fit Solo', and passed the legendary pre-solo simulator check, where all known (and some unknown) emergencies were thrown at you, there was now no turning back. Certain other constraints were also imposed on your first trip, local Flying Orders stating, for example, that you had to have

The mystical light of a late summer's evening bathes two No. 11 Sqn F.6s as they taxy to the runway prior to launching on a dusk sortie.

first flown the T.5 on the day you were scheduled to go solo, and that the weather had to be good. The latter meant a cross-wind of less than ten knots, good visibility and little cloud cover, as you still had not passed your instrument rating test. Occasionally, this meant students would fly the T.5 in the morning and be declared fit solo, only to have the weather deteriorate and force the postponement of the sortie. Yet another dual sortie had to then be completed in the T.5 once the weather had improved. Some unfortunate marginal students reached solo fitness only to be delayed by bad weather. On subsequent dual sorties they failed to attain this standard again, and were never sent solo as a result.

Without stating the obvious, it came as a real shock to walk out to an F.3 on your own, with no one to correct your mistakes, save for the duty instructor in the tower. Keeping an eye on the fuel gauge was now your responsibility, as was

performing a safe landing at the completion of your first trip. This was the ultimate challenge. The F.3 cockpit was just as tight as the 'Tub' – so much so that some pilots had to have the pockets removed from their immersion suits in order to allow them to fit their legs into the foot wells. Taxying out, I remember going through the pre-take-off checks several times to ensure that I'd forgotten nothing. Lining up on the threshold, I had just enough capacity to indulge myself and look over each shoulder at the highly-swept wings. At last I was alone.

Pushing the throttles forward, I let the brakes go and tried desperately to rotate at the right speed. I felt in good hands as my aircraft (XP751) had survived 20 years of frontline flying up to this point in its long career, and I was sure it could manage one more trip – at the time I never thought that just eight days later I'd almost be forced to eject from the

Originally these three Lightnings had departed RAF Valley to fire missiles in the Aberporth range, but at the last minute the weather clamped in and the mission was cancelled. Not wishing to waste the sortie, formation leader John Aldington brought Bob Bees and Dick Coleman into formation for the benefit of the camera.

OCU

The jet pipe area of XP751 after its final flight in October 1986.

much devoted to circuit work. The tricky part came later during the radar phase when your mind was still full of figures, heights and headings from the last intercept – erasing this from your mind in order to concentrate on the landing initially proved a difficult trick to master.

I taxied back to the line, making sure that I'd shut everything down in the correct order. I closed the number two engine down whilst taxiing back, shutting the number one down once I was on the chocks. As I climbed down the ladder my feeling of satisfaction left me as I saw the ground crew covering the main wheels with asbestos blankets to keep the hot brakes from catching fire. I was then informed that I'd not pulled the 'chute, and was asked if there had been a problem. As far as I could recollect I had indeed pulled the 'chute, but on the first solo things tended to be a little blurred. From there, I was unceremoniously wheeled into the boss's office for a sound listening to on my misdemeanours. Thoroughly fed up by having made a mess of my first solo, I was invited to the bar by the rest of the staff to drown my sorrows. Feeling somewhat dejected, I was then put out of my misery when one of the instructors explained that whilst I'd been shutting down, the ground crew had climbed underneath the Lightning and replaced the 'chute that I had in fact deployed on touchdown – it was all a big spoof.

After the excitement of the first solo came two more dual sorties, covering supersonic handling and maximum rate turns – the latter sortie was particularly demanding as you spent 25 minutes carrying out 6g turns in reheat.

On 22 October 1986 I was programmed for two solo sorties – a supersonic handling in the morning, followed by a solo max-rate turn exercise in the afternoon. The morning mission passed by uneventfully until I came in to land. The crosswind had picked up dramatically since I had launched less than an hour before, and as I touched down it was gusting to 35 knots. The Lightning's landing limits were 25 knots in dry conditions and 15 knots for a flooded runway, and I quickly learnt all I needed to know about crosswind landings in 30 seconds as I

same machine, and it would fly its last trip. As soon as I was airborne my first thought was 'now comes the difficult bit of getting this thing back on the ground'. I could just see the mast at Belmont poking through the haze that was slowly enveloping the Lincolnshire wolds like a blanket of cotton wool in the late autumn sunset. At the time, the sortie seemed to pass incredibly slowly, but I can now recollect little of the upper air work. However, I do remember that the landing was uneventful, which was hardly surprising when you take into account that the morning sortie in the T.5 had been pretty

As the sun glints off the tail of XR757, it is clearly evident that this particular Lightning has recently been re-coded.

raced down the tarmac with the stick hard over and boot fully right trying to stay on the runway. I'd already given up on keeping the Lightning on the centreline, and was therefore more than a little relieved when I shut down from that experience.

By mid-afternoon the wind had died down sufficiently enough for me to be sent off again. Each solo sortie was briefed by a QFI, who described in detail what he wanted you to do during the flight, and then quizzed you on a few emergency procedures at the end of the brief. I was detailed to get airborne and head to Spurn Point at an altitude of 5,000 ft, where I was to carry out three or four max-rate turns in both dry power and full reheat. The official technique for performing these manoeuvres was to start at 5,000 ft and reach 500 knots before selecting full reheat and rolling into a turn. When travelling at this speed, you were going too fast to get to the buffet and stay within the aircraft's 6g limit, so the aim instead was to hold the latter figure, and use the excess thrust to gain altitude. As the speed decayed at around 7,000 ft, it was then possible to hold 6g on the light buffet at the maximum angle of attack, whilst still staying in level flight.

It didn't take a rocket scientist to work out that I was only going to be able to remain airborne for a mere 25 minutes unless I gave the low-level turns a miss and stayed in dry power, thus keeping a little fuel in reserve for a bit of circuit flying, which I needed most. So, with my slightly-modified plan in mind, I walked out to XP751 – the aircraft I'd gone solo in eight days previously. The take-off and transit to the area were completed without incident, although I can't say that I was totally 'ahead' of the aeroplane at this early stage in my Lightning career. Commencing the pre-briefed manoeuvres in reheat, I quickly cancelled the 'burner and performed the rest of the sequence in cold power, thus saving the 'gas' for the circuit work. Arriving back over Binbrook, I then completed two circuits, which ran the fuel down to the minimum safe level of 800 lbs a side, before coming into land. Undercarriage down, I called 'Precautionary', pulled the 'chute, retarded the throttles to idle/idle and started braking. The tower suddenly called, '73. No 'Chute'. That was all I needed, following on from the dramas of the morning sortie, but at least the crosswind had by now died down. Nevertheless, the end of the runway started to loom up with alarming speed, so I applied

Recovering back into Binbrook, Simon Braithwaite cruises just above a solid layer of cloud in XR773. This aircraft was amongst the quartet of F.6s handed over to British Aerospace following their retirement from frontline use, and it is today preserved in airworthy condition by the Lightning Flying Club at Exeter airport.

more brake, but took care not to burst the tyres, before safely turning off onto the ORP. The tower now told me that parts of the 'chute cable were hanging from the back of the tailpipe, so deciding that things aft were not as they should be, I stopped where I was, shut down the engines and dismounted to await the arrival of the fire crews.

As I walked to the back of the aircraft I noticed a large hole burnt through the fuselage. This had burned through the 'chute cabling, which is why it never deployed. It was subsequently discovered by the engineering section that a fuel pipe had broken at the rear of the aircraft, leaking fuel into the back end, which ignited when I selected re-heat. The fire was so intense that it burnt through the fire wire

detection system, thus explaining why I had had no cockpit warning of the blaze merrily burning away behind me. Had I flown the sortie as briefed, it is highly likely that the fire would have spread, and without the benefit of the detection system, the first thing I'd have known about it would have been a stiffening of the controls – I'd have been forced to eject on only my third solo sortie. And the aircraft would have joined several others abandoned off the coast of Spurn Point over the preceding 25 years.

Apparently, my course progress report folder was annotated to denote that 'Flt Lt Black had been rather shaken by the events of 22 October 1986'. My next sortie was, however, an uneventful solo, prior to starting the instrument phase. After a

LAST OF THE LIGHTNINGS

further four trips you took a full instrument test (staged over two sorties), culminating in a White Rating, which meant that you could land if the cloud base was above 400 ft.

After the intense work load associated with instrument flying, formation keeping (including low-level tactical work) and tail chasing provided a welcome break during the next phase of the syllabus. It goes without saying that the aeroplane was a delight to fly in close formation, being both stable and smooth throughout the speed range. The only tricky part came when close-formation take-offs were performed, as the view across the cockpit wasn't that brilliant. Possessing one of the last true flight lines in the RAF, Binbrook was a delight to taxy out from as there were no HASs present which could confuse you as to the location of your leader. On the line you could easily see the rest of your formation, and the use of the radio was hardly needed. If anyone had a problem on start up, you could see exactly what his progress was, and if he needed to run for the spare.

With all the formation ready, closing the canopy was normally the visual sign used to indicate that you were ready to taxy. On a wet winter's day extreme care was needed on the runway line up as the aircraft could easily slide, with disastrous consequences if there were already other aircraft lined up. Once lined up, the leader then gave the 'wind up' signal, which again took the form of a circular motion of the hand with the forefinger extended. The pilot of the number two aircraft

Having taken off from RAF Akrotiri some five hours earlier, the memory of sun and sea seem a million miles away and reality strikes home as the three-ship formation let down into Binbrook – forecast: low cloud, wind and rain!

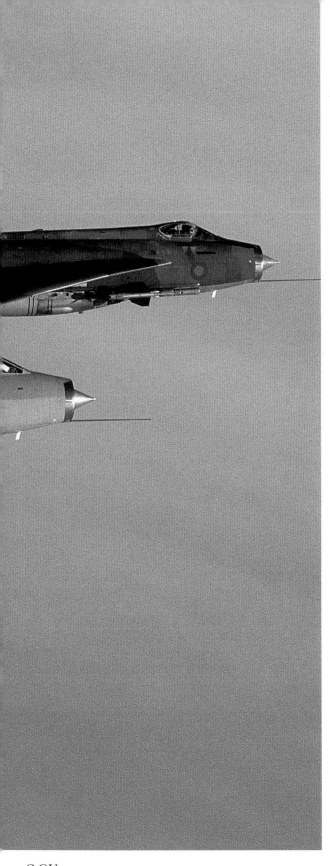

would then open his throttles, giving a thumb's up to indicate when he was ready to roll. Having acknowledged the signal, the leader would motion for brake release by a simple nod of the head, before running up to full power to check his temperatures and RPM, prior to again throttling back to allow the number two some leeway. The latter then divided his attention between watching the leader and keeping on his own side of the runway as the two Lightnings accelerated down the tarmac – with practice you could look ahead and watch the leader in your peripheral vision.

Once airborne, you then concentrated solely on the leader, watching his undercarriage for when he applied his brakes to stop the wheels from spinning – this was the signal to simultaneously raise your gear also. If reheat had been used on take-off, the leader would nod his head sharply to indicate that he was 'cutting the 'burner'. Once airborne, you either stayed in close if you were perhaps climbing through cloud, or broke away into battle formation – the latter was known as a 'Playtex', as you literally used to 'lift and separate'. In formation, you flew on pre-briefed references – for echelon this was with the trailing edge of the wing lined up on the tailplane. When slotted into the correct echelon position, the jet pipes of the lead Lightning were 'squared off'. Trying to judge your lateral spacing was slightly more difficult, however. Three feet was the optimal wing tip clearance for display flying. Because of control problems overlapping wing tips was banned. Flying in line astern, the clearance was around six feet, with the number two staying far enough below the lead Lightning so as to let the latter's jetwash pass harmlessly over the top of his tailplane and rudder. As all LTF take-offs were performed in dry power, the problem of accidentally deselecting reheat during the take-off didn't arise.

With these few trips completed, it was back to general handling prior to tackling the mid-course handling check. This sortie was used by the LTF instructors to gauge a student's progress following the completion of 25 to 30 hours on type – it was normally flown with the boss of the Flight, who was a QFI. It provided a thorough test of all the skills

All three aircraft are carrying live Red Top missiles in this shot, and waiting for a range slot that was eventually cancelled due to poor weather.

learned by the pilot so far, and always finished with a no notice practice diversion to a local airfield following the declaration of a simulated emergency. Having successfully passed this vital sortie, it was back to ground school for a week's radar theory and weapons system lectures. Prior to undertaking a radar sortie, lengthy briefs were given by the instructors on handling the radar, and its associated missiles – both the Firestreak and the Red Top were covered by the LTF, but gunnery was left to the squadrons as no Flight aircraft were so equipped.

Many hours were devoted to the principles of basic radar theory, intercept theory and aircraft performance, with much use being made of the simulator. Indeed, every sortie was first flown in the 'Box', prior to being tackled in the air. Naturally, much emphasis was placed on the radar phase of the course, as the Lightning pilot's 'bread and butter' was the 'head down' intercept. In theory, most pilots could pick up a target on radar, keep it on the scope and then 'plug in the 'burners' and chase after it when it came within missile range. Reality required a little more skill and finesse to achieve success every time, however. Imagine yourself at night, or in cloud, leading your wingman, who has lost all his instruments, onto a tanker – these were the situations where you earned your keep, performing a smooth, radar-controlled, join up in such a way as to allow even a novice pilot to stay on your wing.

Initial radar sorties were very basic in their content, with the target (normally a high-fatigue/houred F.6) holding the same heading, height and speed – the delights of target evasion came later. However, within six months of first using the radar, a pilot would be expected to cope with any evasion in height, heading or speed employed by the contact. Early radar sorties were extremely taxing, and many students became saturated with the high workload.

Leading this formation in 'his' personal aircraft was Flt Lt Colin Rae, a former Navy Wessex pilot who had 'seen the light' and transferred to the RAF. This particular mission was a two v one combat sortie which had started with a close formation vic take-off. Transiting over a less than clear North Sea, the two opponents have come into close prior to the combat commencing. Ironically, the nose sections of both of these aircraft have been preserved.

This shot aptly sums up the term 'all-weather fighter'. Flight Commander Sqn Ldr Paul Cooper (a former RAFG F.2A pilot) returns to the line after a standard intercept sortie. The only real weather limits placed on the Lightning revolved around runway crosswinds.

Some pilots could fly the Lightning, but couldn't interpret the radar, whilst others could work the radar but were at the limit of their capacity when it came to flying the aircraft. After I finished the course, the next two students who arrived exhibited these very traits, and with their usual black sense of humour, the LTF staff suggested that rather than 'chop' them both, they should always be paired together in the T.5 at squadron level! They were both eventually suspended from training.

The LTF had a reputation for being hard on its pupils, but if ever there was an aircraft that deserved respect in the air, then the Lightning was it. Indeed, it is true to say that towards the end of its service career the Lightning was being operated in a fashion that exceeded its original design specification, as attempting to fly the aircraft whilst having your head 'stuck' in the radar tube – yet still managing the fuel and weapons system – required a new, and as yet unfound, skill. To achieve a simulated missile launch with sole reference to radar was (and still is) no small feat in a single-seat fighter. Even harder to perform was a visual identification on a target at night, or in cloud, which required you to arrive at

'Sandbagging' with the squadron boss in the T.5 gave me a chance to photograph 'BG' prior to a four-ship flypast. The term 'sandbagging' stems from Royal Flying Corps days when ballast was added on solo flights to keep the centre of gravity in the correct place.

Looking every inch a thoroughbred fighter, 'BC' is seen against a superb cumulus backdrop – notice the wingtip vortices trailing in the aircraft's wake.

the minimum separation distance of 300 yards using radar alone. This was the Lightning's principle peacetime role – to 'identify targets, unknown, day or night in all-weathers 365 days a year'. The 'vis-ident' procedure involved closing in on the target to a distance of about a mile, before gently easing in towards the aircraft to a distance of 300 yards. Whilst with the LTF you always simulated that the target was in cloud, or you were flying at night, which meant that you only looked out of the cockpit at minimum range and, if visual, joined in close formation.

Having just got to grips with the aircraft's start up and pre-take-off checks, it was now back to square

one with an even more complex list of weapon and pre-attack checks to memorize. Starting on the ground with the walk-round check, it was no longer permissible to simply ignore the weapons pack prior to climbing into the cockpit. For example, if Red Top rounds were fitted you now had to check the general condition of the missile's body and seeker head. Only on the squadrons would you fly with live missiles for QRA, or on missile firing exercises, and these were fitted with delicate bakolite guidance fins that were absent from the training rounds. With Firestreak, it was a necessary to check the ammonia bottle and the accumulator pressure gauge fitted in the weapons pack, as well as ensuring that the

A last photo call before the Lightning was withdrawn from frontline service. Evident is the vertical twin jet arrangement, compared with the more conventional horizontal tail pipes of the Tornado F.3.

OCU

seeker head was devoid of cracks, and that the round was free of leaks.

On entering the cockpit it soon became religion to check that the trigger was 'safe' and the radar switched off – in reality air defence aircraft rarely fly with live weapons on peacetime missions, but this routine nevertheless taught you to treat both aspects of the Lightning with respect. Once seated in the cockpit, a new control then came into operation in the form of the radar hand-controller. Located immediately behind the throttles, this device was truly a work of art, having apparently been designed by someone who made devices for use by disabled people. It was way ahead of its time, and incredibly user-friendly, the unit consisting of a small rectangular metal box assembly into which slid a cylindrical tube onto which was a hand lever. Through the manipulation of this lever, all radar controls could be operated with a single hand, so that everything moved in a logical fashion. For example, pulling the cylinder in and out drove the radar scanner up or down, which by today's

standards was very limited in its movement, covering just +27° to –8°. Moving the handle left or right had a similar effect on the target acquisition marker, whilst two small thumb wheels on top of the handle scrolled the marker up or down the scope, the second wheel controlling the radar gain, or sensitivity. The radar was activated by the manipulation of several small switches, which were easily accessible under the box – these changed the range scale and operated various other modes. The hand-controller was a marvellous piece of equipment.

Moving around the cockpit in the two-seater, the next item to catch your attention was the radar display, known affectionately as the 'four-inch torture tube'. The small screen was normally covered with a large rubber 'boot' that could be folded flat when not in use – its purpose was to mask the screen from the sun's glare. Next to the radar was the rudimentary gunsight, which was usually adorned with a dayglo sticker that served to remind the pilot of the Lightning's individual

airframe g limit. To the right of the main instrument panel was the armament indicator panel and the armament selector switches.

Having rattled through the now almost familiar checks, the start sequence took only a few minutes to complete. From day one of the radar phase, the student had to add the pre-take-off weapon checks to his taxying out routine, which consisted principally of a brief radar test. With this successfully completed, you now at least had some idea of the transmitter's operability. The Ferranti radar was, by the 1980s, 'steam-driven', looking somewhat out of place alongside a modern track-while-scan, raid-assessment mode and phased-array radars. Modern radars stay fixed in position with the scan being electronic, thus making hydraulic drives and scanners banging away under your feet a

thing of the past. Indeed, the only 'interface' between the Lightning's radar and its weapons system was the pilot's brain – today, weapons computers deal with all possible threats.

Having already completed a myriad of systems checks, the pilot would level the Lightning off at height and calibrate the radar in order to check that it was accurately displaying the aircraft's altitude.

The purpose of the many medium level radar sorties flown whilst on the LTF was to teach you how to roll out one-and-a-half miles behind the target in a controlled manner, and either 'fire' a missile or close in for a 'vis-ident'. For the early sorties both the target and fighter would head toward the north-east and contact Boulmer Radar for intercepts between 10,000 and 35,000 ft. These sorties would be performed in visual conditions,

With the APC complete, two soot-stained F.6s return to Akrotiri and prepare for the break to land. XR769 was the last Lightning lost by the RAF prior to the aircraft's service retirement.

OCU

85

A close-up of Flt Lt Marc Ims (now a Harrier GR.7 QWI) peering down the radar boot in search of our tanker.

thus allowing the student to obtain visual on the target, which would serve to and reassure him that there really was an aircraft out there! Certain parameters were briefed prior to take-off between the fighter and target, with the former maintaining a speed of 0.85 Mach and the latter 0.75 Mach. Initially, the target would hold a pre-briefed height of say 25,000 ft, and the fighter could then fly either 1,000 ft above or below this ceiling. With the Lightning's radar capable of searching in pulse-mode only, it was normally best to stay below the target and look up, thus avoiding ground or sea returns. Initial subsonic intercepts were always flown with

the radar 'unlocked' – that is to say the pilot had to keep illuminating the target by moving the radar scanner elevation up or down.

The first practice intercept demonstrated on the LTF was the 180° attack, which saw the target flying towards you on a reciprocal heading displaced laterally by eight miles to the left or right. The Lightning's turn radius at this particular height and speed was known to be four miles, so as long as you started in the right place, you would roll out behind the contact line astern at a distance of one-and-a-half miles.

As the sun sets in the west, Australian exchange pilot Dick Coleman closes in on my left wing.

Never afraid of water, the Lightning made short work of the rain-sodden Binbrook runway on a near-daily basis.

When I took this photograph of XP693 in late 1992 I had just about run out of ideas for a new angle on the Lightning. therefore, in an effort to try something different I asked the Hawk pilot to go as close as he could to the left wingtip of the aircraft, and using a wide-angle lens, I exploited the image distortion and the weak winter light to produce this dramatic shot.

Training for the radar phase was either confined to the simulator, or the student had unrestricted use of a device called 'Bill Beck's Magic Box'. Although the latter sounds like some high-tech piece of computer equipment, it was, in truth, simply a cardboard box with a slit cut out, into which you placed a selection of cards. Each intercept angle followed a known track, which could be memorized and then used to form a reference in flight. For example, the blip (track) for a 180° intercept starts at around 20° off the nose at 25 miles, then moves to 25° at 20 miles, then 32° at 15 miles, before finally arriving at 40° at 12 miles – the turning point. Thus, having memorized the ideal curve, a student could then assess if the intercept was ideal, tight or slack. If the intercept was tight (i.e. less than eight miles displaced), the final turn key of 40° off at 12 miles wouldn't work. To adjust for this, the pilot had to recognize that he was too close and turn away until he hit the ideal displacement, then turn back onto the original heading.

Although this manoeuvre may sound simple in

black and white, try carrying it out at 30,000 ft whilst tightly strapped to an ejector seat, wearing a restrictive rubber exposure suit and locked into an aluminium box. Add to this the simple matter of physically flying the aircraft, coping with the GCI talking to you, and constantly having to check on your home base weather and position, and you should begin to get a feel for the task that faced the Lightning student on these first harrowing intercept sorties.

As with the tight attack, the opposite applies to a slack intercept – i.e. a target which was over eight miles displaced. Here, the pilot had to turn into the target and wait until he estimated that he was eight miles from it before resuming his original heading.

Without further complicating matters, these turn keys only worked if the pre-briefed fighter and target speeds remained constant. With 'Bill Beck's Magic Box', each intercept was traced onto a card which could be inserted into the cardboard receptacle. As you pushed the card down, a slit in the box revealed the 'blip', thus giving the student an opportunity to try and identify the type of intercept profile that needed to be flown – a cheap, but very effective, aid to learning intercept geometry.

One of the major limitations of the Lightning from an avionics point of view was the radar's poor detection range against medium level targets. On the LTF most of the aeroplanes carried a Luneburg lens radar reflector located in the seeker head of a Red Top missile, which made the average target pick up range somewhere in the region of 20 to 25 miles, as opposed to 18 to 20 miles on non-equipped aircraft. These early sorties were extremely tense, as you struggled first to locate the target and then work out its heading, whilst at the same time assessing if he was on the right keys in order to perform an interception. Additionally, you needed to quickly calculate the height difference between you and your target, before either climbing or descending to within 1,000 ft of his ceiling. This was for two reasons – first, to give the missile less work to do, and second, to make life easier holding the target in radar contact. The closer you came to the target, the more you had to raise or lower the radar scanner to hold him in the beam – the greater the height difference, the harder this became.

Having reached your final turn position, which was going to roll you out perfectly line astern of the target, it was now time to get on with the serious work. As the final turn was a known trajectory, in theory the 'blip' should have followed a set pattern. However, if you started the turn and the target wasn't adhering to the pattern you had memorized, either the target was tighter, or you had assessed his heading wrongly. Again, it was now a question of playing the turn to get yourself back on the ideal path. At this stage mission workload was extremely high as you were having to look down into the radar every 30° in order to update yourself. The LTF teaching was to treat the radar scope as another instrument, and therefore check the scope as part of an overall instrument scan. It was abundantly easy to become mesmerized by the AI.23, especially when things went wrong.

Once you got in behind the target you could either lock him up and fire a missile, shoot unlocked or lock and close for a 'vis-ident'. The latter was a

XS904 holds the distinction of being the last Lightning to visit RAF Germany, as prior to No. 19 Sqn's disbandment in 1992, it was the star of the static display at Wildenrath – it is seen here on its way back to Warton after the weekend event. Note the blue No. 19 Sqn 'zap' just above the fin flash.

Taxying past an inert Red Top-equipped F.6, the No. 11 Sqn T.5 sets off on a dreaded night dual sortie.

slow and painstaking exercise that required a great deal of care and attention to be paid to the instruments. For this reason, most of the transits to and from the 'play area' were flown in radar trail, with the student locked on behind the target so as not to waste valuable fuel.

After a couple of radar sorties another general handling trip was flown with a QFI, but this time at night. These were fairly traumatic as most students only had about seven hours total night flying, accrued on the Hawk and Jet Provost. Night formation work was left to the squadrons to teach. Compared to modern aircraft, the Lightning's landing lights were fairly ineffective and prone to failure, which only served to raise your anxiety level! Night emergencies required the use of a torch so as to allow you to signal to your wingman the nature

of your problem should you have lost radio communication. Following the night dual you were sent on a night solo, which usually comprised a practise diversion to a local airfield followed by instrument approaches and circuits at Binbrook. The night dual was a fairly important part of the syllabus, as a squadron pilot might have flown up to 25 per cent of his annual 220 hours after sunset – a degree of competence was therefore essential. Should you have been unlucky enough to complete the LTF course in the winter months, then it was possible to do some of the radar work at night, as more often than not, the last take-off would be at around 16:00, which guaranteed a night recovery during December and January.

With the 'qualified night' stamp in your logbook, it was back to the radar phase, and all its associated delights. Once you had mastered the standard 180° attack, it was time to move on to the 150°, 120° and 90° profiles, these different intercepts being the angular difference between your heading and the target. At first all the headings of the target were known, but as the course progressed they became 'Intercepts Unknown'. Once in the 'play area' somewhere over the North Sea, GCI would tell the target aircraft to take up a heading between say 180° and 270°. After the distance between the two aircraft had increased to about 30 miles, GCI would chip in with 'Target. Turn right 150°, plus or minus 30°'. This brief communiqué should have sufficiently confused the student as to the true intercept geometry.

One of the LTF staff tried in vain to teach me a simple way (in his estimation, at least) of calculating the inbound heading of a contact, but I never understood it, and it seemed more complicated than waiting till you detected him on radar! Calculation of target heading using the AIRPASS equipment involved watching the change of displacement over a five-mile period. If the target change of displacement was zero over this distance then you could assume

you were on a 180° attack, and that his heading was simply the opposite to yours. If the displacement was one to one-and-a-half miles, then he was on a 150° attack, whilst up to three miles and over would indicate a 90° attack profile, flown either left to right or vice versa. Bearing in mind that the longest range detection you were ever likely to get was in the order of 25 miles, as a student you really had your work cut out.

The closing speed was roughly 18 miles per minute, so the time from initial detection to turning in behind the target was somewhere in the order of one minute. In that time you needed to calculate the heading and then see if it was on the ideal track for your calculated intercept, before adjusting it as required. It was essential to take out the height difference as soon as the initial heading assessment had been done, as this allowed you to be within roughly 2,000 ft of the contact's height at a distance of ten miles – well set up for the final height check. At this distance you also noted the scanner elevation and multiplied it by ten, thus giving you the target height in thousands of feet.

To ease the student's workload, all stages of the

Sandwiched between the moon and the sun, Steve Hunt finishes his 'vis-ident' and joins up close.

'Contact'. Accelerating away in search of his target, the pilot 'plugs in' full reheat during a dusk interception.

intercept were broken down into sequences, with initial detection being made with the autopilot engaged, which held the Lightning rock steady in both height and heading. This was particularly important when working out the target heading, as any wandering of your own course would mean your calculations were invalid. Prior to each radar sortie being flown, the target height parameters were briefed – you therefore knew the maximum and minimum levels for the intercept. This also meant you could position the radar scanner accurately in the lead up to detection, thus avoiding a fruitless search of vast chunks of empty sky. As you and the target turned towards each other, GCI would give you what was known as 'Bravo control' – the target bearing and its range, updated every 15 seconds, which at least gave you a rough idea of where to look. As soon as you turned to face the target the first task was to start the stopwatch – if all other systems failed, at least you had something tangible to work from. Having assessed heading and crossing angle, you then attempted to put yourself onto the ideal turn keys, whilst at the same time sorting out the all-important height separation for a preferred

attack from below so as to give the radar the best chance of acquiring the target.

Once you were into the final turn, all previous suspicions about the type of intercept you should be flying were either confirmed or dispelled, for as you 'went round the corner', the moment of truth arrived! If your calculations were correct, the 'blip' stayed on the right keys and everything worked smoothly. If not, it was necessary to 'fudge' the turn and make allowances for your errors, whilst trying desperately to remember what heading you thought the target was on prior to rolling out. If your assessment was correct the target remained stationary, but if you had got it wrong it began to drift. Making sure you regained any lost speed, the main priority was to ensure that the aircraft was under control. Once in behind the target you were faced with two options – either shoot it down or identify and shadow it. If the former course of action was chosen, you visually acquired your target and fired off a round, but if you couldn't physically see your enemy, radar lock-on was the only option left, notwithstanding the limitation that the missile could not acquire its target in cloud. For a locked

firing, the radar displayed three differing sizes of circle, indicating the range firing brackets.

At this point in the Lightning conversion the level of stress felt by the student was perhaps best described by the following quote taken from the LTF line book – 'The best thing that could happen to the T.5 is that someone crashes it into the simulator'.

'Vis-idents' covered the visual identification of a target initially through the use of radar, prior to the pilot closing in on the contact for a final lock-on with the Mark One eyeball'. In peacetime, the minimum range you could close on the target aircraft on radar was 300 yards, after which the system would normally break lock, and you would be forced to either visually acquire the 'blip' or break off the interception. As the primary peacetime role of the Lightning force was to police UK airspace, a great deal of time and effort was spent perfecting these 'vis-ident' manoeuvres. On the ground, students were encouraged to read recognition manuals so as to be able to identify both civil and military aircraft whilst airborne. Initially, the LTF taught 'vis-idents' by flying sorties at medium altitudes below the target, before moving onto the more difficult low-level approaches.

Although the Lightning's AI.23 system could lock on to the target, it only gave you a range and an azimuth, but not the overtaking speed. Therefore, as you closed behind the target, it was vital you accurately calculated its speed so as to ensure that your approach was flown in a safe and controlled manner. Although the technique employed was

basic, it was nevertheless reliable. As soon as you achieved a radar lock, you hit the stopwatch and timed the rate of closure over 15 seconds. Thus, if you closed on the contact by 250 yards in this time, it meant that the target was flying 30 knots slower than you were. Likewise, if you covered 1000 yards, it meant that you were going 120 knots faster than your opponent. As a second check, at 900 yards you attempted to fly co-speed with the target in order to reconfirm your calculations. A further safety constraint saw you call out the target speed on the radio, to which the instructor replied with the correct answer. In reality, the manufacturer's minimum radar lock range was 500 yards, so as you got nearer you looked out to try and get a visual. At medium level you aimed to be low, line astern, at 300 yards, prior to calling visual and then closing up. A successful outcome to the intercept hinged on the pilot exercising every ounce of his newly-acquired skill in flying the Lightning accurately on instruments. Whilst closing in, every small movement was exaggerated, and all control inputs had to be restricted to plus or minus 1°, or plus or minus five knots. Of course the daylight/clear air 'vis-idents' performed on the LTF were only a precursor to the far more taxing night work performed without the aid of navigation lights by the squadrons.

A mid-course handling sortie with an instructor in the T.5 was then flown (just to check that you hadn't forgotten the basics), before progressing to low-level intercepts. Here, the radar was really out of its depth, but with a little help from GCI, it was surprising what could be achieved. In the low-level environment the aircraft had many drawbacks, but also a few plus points. As mentioned earlier, the radar was a pulse only set of the true 1950s fashion, making it excellent for finding a ship or an oil rig in the North Sea, but rather less adept at locating a bomber skimming in over the waves at 250 ft and 500 knots. Allied to its poor radar performance was the Lightning's horrendous appetite for fuel when 'down on the deck', especially at speeds in excess of 500 knots. When at low-level dashing along at 600 knots, the aircraft devoured 400 lbs of fuel per

'BZ' was one of a pair of T.5s held on strength by No. 11 Sqn, and is seen here heading east for a weekend stopover in Cyprus.

minute, and if this speed was sustained your CAP time would be restricted to just 12 minutes before you had to return to Binbrook with just the regulation minimum of 1,600 lbs for recovery. Another big drawback with the Lightning was that it lacked any autonomous navigation aids whilst operating over the sea, the TACAN tending not to work at low-level once you had gone beyond a distance of 40 miles from Binbrook, and the radar only proving useful for 'painting' an outline of the coast if you were heading in a westerly direction.

However, perhaps the worst feature of all was the aircraft's altimeter system – the T.5 didn't even come equipped with a radar altimeter! The rule of thumb used when working with the altimeter was at 400 knots the system error was the same value as the speed. Hence, at 2,000 ft proper, you needed to subtract your speed and fly at 1,600 ft indicated, which would then actually translate to the former figure! Unfortunately this was not a linear

calculation, and as your speed increased so did the error. Therefore, at 500 knots it was 700 ft whilst at 600 knots it had increased to 1,500 ft, which would mean flying at 500 ft indicated to achieve 2,000 ft true. The real difficulty came when flying at 1,000 ft at night, the minimum laid down altitude allowed over the sea either at night or in cloud. If you flew a 600-knot target profile, you actually had to make the altimeter read –500 ft – no wonder many people thought that Lightning pilots' were certifiable!

On the plus side, most of the attacks at this height were of the 90° type, and most crews tended not to look for interceptors approaching from their beam. Any errors in intercept geometry could also be quickly solved using the tremendous overtake available with the Lightning. The low-level intercepts were always flown using Staxton Wold GCI station, located in the Vale of Pickering. Close links were forged between the controllers at Staxton and the Binbrook pilots, as most low-level sorties were flown south of Flamborough Head, a short distance from the coast. Normally, the fighter would sit 1,000 to 5,000 ft above the target and try to place the radar scanner in the rough position of the target. It then became a bit of an art to reduce the radar gain so that the tube wasn't swamped with returns from the sea. As you moved the radar scanner down, so you had to wind the gain down and reduce radar sensitivity. With the maximum look down of the radar limited to −10°, it was best to stay 1,000 ft higher, otherwise it would go out of scan.

GCI would try to set you up on a 90° attack, crossing the nose at between three to five miles – the ideal range was exactly four miles. In an effort to keep the fuel burn as low as possible, the target flew at 300 knots and the fighter at 360, thus giving you 'bags of spare poke' if you needed to accelerate quickly. In practice, as long as the target flew across your nose at the distance previously mentioned, you could 'play' the final turn in order to roll out behind the contact at an ideal separation of one-and-a-half miles. During the final turn, a descent was made to target height plus 500 ft. Now, more than ever, it was time to concentrate on your instrument flying,

being so close to the sea. Once behind the target, you performed the same procedure as if you were flying at medium level, either firing a simulated missile or closing in for a 'vis-ident'. With the target flying at 1,000 ft, or 250 ft by day, all 'idents' were flown from above, with the fighter offset either to the right or left, depending on tactical considerations.

With the low-level phase now completed, it was time to fold the radar boot away and indulge in some visual air combat. Several dual sorties were flown to get you used to putting the aircraft on the g limit, with great care being taken not to exceed the airframe's 6g limit through too rapid a build up of speed. Sortie duration was now down to absurd levels, with some trips as short as ten minutes being logged which necessitated that combat take place above the airfield. Most of the missions were flown dual at this stage in the course, although one or two were performed in the F.3.

Having by now logged around 40 hours flying during approximately 80 sorties, the end of the course was in sight. A short phase of low-level evasion was next on the syllabus, often flown within visual range of the airfield. Two Lightnings would

Sqn Ldr 'Furz' Lloyd banks the distinctively-marked No. 5 Sqn flagship low over Spurn Point just prior to the unit's disbandment.

Parked in front of the No. 11 Sqn hangars, the unit's flagship also donned a full-colour fin (in traditional black) towards the end of 1987.

get airborne and head east for three minutes, prior to setting up a visual CAP over a major land feature like the Covenham Reservoir – its ease of visual acquisition ensured accurate navigation. The designated target aircraft would then split off, only to return from a different direction hell-bent on taking an unseen shot at the student. With the radar performance of no use, it was simply a case of keeping the visual look out going for the entire duration of the sortie. If you had an early 'pick up', you could try and use ground cover to sneak up on the target, but if he saw you first, it was a case of going for a close aboard pass, and then pulling into the vertical to kill your speed with height, before trying to get round the back of him.

To complete the course, a dual sortie was flown with the most experienced weapons instructor on the LTF. This sortie could see you employing a number of your recently-learned skills whilst flying a high-, medium- or low-level intercept profile. At the end of the sortie, the target would announce a simulated emergency, meaning that the student would have to escort him home for a pairs approach and recovery. Having passed the final sortie, most students already knew which squadron they had been assigned to, and duly set off on the short walk to locate a new Flying Clothing locker. As with finishing at the TWU, a graduate of the LTF would imagine that all his troubles were now behind him as he had achieved the goal of frontline flying – nothing could have been further from the truth, as air-to-air refuelling, gunnery and lights out 'vis-idents' all lay ahead. Typically, it would be another full year before the student would at last be classed a fully 'operational' Lightning pilot.

CHAPTER 3

Death of a Lightning

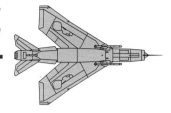

Ask anyone what the Lightning was famous for, and the chances are they will either tell you its amazing vertical climb performance, or its high accident rate. It can't be denied that the RAF lost a lot of Lightnings in the early years. It must, however, be taken in context that here was a revolutionary aircraft in many respects. The air force had gone from flying the subsonic Hunter to the Mach 2.0+ Lightning in one step. It also remained in the frontline for almost 30 years, beating all longevity records for previous RAF fighters. By the mid-1980s, most of the engineering problems associated with the aircraft had been ironed out, and the Lightning enjoyed a safety rate no worse than any other Western fighter. True, by this stage in its long career the Lightning was no longer regularly involved in the potentially more hazardous role of low-level interceptions over land, some of its remaining mission profiles were no less demanding. A large part of the aeroplane's life was now spent low down over the sea, often at night – hitting a seagull at 600 knots was enough to spoil anyone's day.

During its final months of operations, one of the last F.6s lost fell victim to a freak accident during an annual gunnery training camp. The aircraft involved (XR763) was being flown on 1 July 1987 by Flt Lt 'Charlie' Chan – a young first tour pilot with No. 5 Sqn – on a live firing pass on the banner during his unit's last APC to Cyprus with the Lightning a million to one accident occurred. During one 'hot' pass, his bullets hit the top spreader bar wheel

(which weighed a hefty one pound) on the banner, and this detached and headed for his Lightning. Through some fluke, the wheel was ingested by the aircraft without damaging the radar bullet, the pilot hearing a metallic 'clunk' as the disc was 'swallowed' by the number one engine. The latter immediately seized, so Chan shut it down, before quickly steering the stricken aeroplane in the direction of Akrotiri. With the number one Avon shut down, and the number two left at a fixed power setting, he duly headed for home. However, the damage inflicted on the bottom engine was so bad that parts of it had been ingested by the second engine, and on short finals Chan felt the thrust drop and the aircraft 'sag'. He tried selecting 'burner, but this had no effect as the jet pipe temperature simply went off the clock, so his only remaining option was for a 'Martin-Baker' let down, which was a total success. Ironically, the aircraft had only just returned to No. 5 Sqn after having endured months of work being carried out on it as part of the life extension programme – in this case its extended service life could be measured in days rather than months! Its life extension was rather short lived.

Three months prior to this crash on 19 March 1987, Flt Lt Barry Lennon had ejected from LTF F.3 XP707, which therefore became the 23rd, and last, F.3 lost in 23 years of service. Having been selected as the last display pilot for the Lightning, Lennon had just started his pre-season work-up phase when things went very wrong for him during an early sortie in the Binbrook overhead. Unbeknown to

Despite the great age (and technology) gap, the Lightning could still pull a few punches when it came to 'mixing it' with high tech fly-by-wire American fighters.

him, fuel had inexplicably remained trapped in the aircraft's ventral tank long after it should have emptied during the course of the flight. This caused a drastic change in the aircraft's centre of gravity – with disastrous results. As Lennon pushed inverted, the aeroplane departed controlled flight and he was forced to eject, with the unfortunate XP707 crashing in a field a few hundred yards from Binbrook's boundary fence. The aircraft had led a very full life, having served with five frontline units, No. 226 OCU and finally the LTF, following its delivery to the RAF in November 1963. It had also been one of the few Wattisham F.3s to escape the cutter's torch when the Suffolk-based wing disbanded in 1975. Following the crash, only XP707's tail remained recognizable as having belonged to a Lightning.

By April 1988 spirits were high in the No. 11 Sqn crew room as the flying was excellent, with lots of air combat and low-level training with dedicated ground attack aircraft to be had. All this was tinged with a good deal of sadness, however, for we all knew that in four weeks' time the squadron would be declared non-operational. We were, of course, the focus of much media attention, with journalists constantly visiting the base – it seemed everyone

wanted to be there at the end. Aviation enthusiasts from across the globe also knew that this really was the end for Britain's best-loved jet fighter, after several previous threats to its existence.

April 11, 1988 dawned much as any other day at Binbrook during that spring, but for once the weatherman had forecast clear blue skies and unlimited visibility. I'd spent the previous day telephoning all the other UK-based fighter squadrons looking for 'trade' – adversaries for combat. I was detailed to be the leader of a four-ship of Lightnings, and our 'playground' was going to be the spacious North Sea training area. As a bonus, we had a Victor tanker on task with enough fuel for us and any adversaries we might work against. A quick call to No. 74 Sqn (unique in being the only operators of the all-American F-4J(UK) Phantom IIs in the RAF) at Wattisham found them keen to test their mettle against the last of the 'single-seaters', so following a check on timings, it soon looked as though we had a workable plan.

We would get airborne first and go straight to the Victor rendezvous point, where we would fill our tanks to full. The 'Tigers' would then take on fuel and start their attack on our CAP. Running quickly through the mandatory briefing guide over the telephone, I made sure that both the F-4 mission leader and I were conversing on the same wavelength, and happy with the plan.

Prior to each sortie being flown, a number of points have to be covered, including the radio frequencies, who is simulating what threat and what armament is to be carried. In the latter area we were most definitely the underdogs, pitted against a potent, if somewhat uncharismatic, fighting machine, which boasted an awesome weapons suite when compared with our 'steam-driven' F.6s. The Phantom II crews were also blessed with a sophisticated radar warning receiver, which could easily pick up our AI.23D, whilst we had nothing to detect their long-range AWG-10 system. All we could do was rely on a combination of effective GCI and slick radar work. The best we could manage was to employ a form of decoy tactic at a range that we thought would fool them into launching their Sparrow missiles prematurely. Of course this ploy relied heavily on pure luck, as we had no positive means of knowing if we were being illuminated at the time due to our lack of RWR. The ace up our sleeves, however, was that we carried chaff, which could be employed to break their radar lock, and

thus deny them the chance to shoot at us from head on. Unlike the chaff pods fitted integrally into today's combat aircraft, our dispensers were neither self-programming or computer-driven – we carried into combat as many bundles of chaff as the ground crew could manage to stuff into the airbrakes after the Lightning had started up! This also meant that its deployment was a 'one-shot deal'. When you selected airbrakes out, the whole lot was dispensed in one foul swoop. In order to make the most effective use of our four lots of chaff, we had to work to a pre-briefed plan once engaged in combat. I also made a mental note on the briefing guide to instruct my formation on the recovery procedure once the air combat was over – just as it is very important to complete all the pre-attack checks, it is equally as important to do all the post-attack checks. Nothing could be more embarrassing than to not use your chaff over the sea, and then on recovery to base break into the circuit, 'pop' the airbrakes out and dump it all over your own airfield! With all the preparations complete, all that now remained was for me to make up the briefing slides for the next day's sortie.

After the obligatory weather brief on the 11th, I had enough time to prepare my mission, 'phone the

Just about to 'plug' into the Victor tanker, XR769 prepares to take on fuel for the last time – the aircraft had less than 20 minutes to live.

adversaries and check that the tanker was still available. In my formation was Flt Lt Dick Coleman, an exchange pilot from the Royal Australian Air Force who had flown Mirage IIIOs prior to his posting on to Lightnings – he had passed the LTF course without any dramas, unlike his predecessor (also a former Mirage pilot) who had failed to make the grade, claiming that we 'Brits' were crazy operating the Lightning in the way that we did. In the second element was Flt Lt Alan 'Porky' Page, an experienced Binbrook operator, and Flg Off Derek 'Grinner' Smith, a young pilot who had recently joined us from No. 5 Sqn.

As midday approached, we all grabbed a sandwich, donned our exposure suits and headed off for the briefing room. Despite it being a warm spring day, the sea temperature in our area of operations was still only around 8°C following the long, cold, winter. At this time of year you would have been lucky to survive more than an hour in the water unless you were wearing the correct protective clothing. Although the immersion suit was a cumbersome item of kit, all Lightning pilots soon got used to wearing it – indeed, they were a standard item of clothing for all Binbrook pilots between September and mid-May. The minimum sea temperature for discarding the suit was 10°C, but this is still extremely cold, and even in summer it was a good idea to wear the immersion suit when flying at night. The No. 11 Sqn briefing room was located behind the fire doors that divided the unit hangar, and unlike its modern equivalent, lacked high-tech visual display aids – pilots had to make do with a simple projector, bare walls and a chalkboard. Once settled for the brief, I covered in detail the transit to the tanker, how and in what order we would do the join and what fuel load we would take. On this day there was no spare aircraft available, so I briefed my number three that if my aircraft went unserviceable he had the lead.

Amongst the aircraft that comprised our formation we had the black-finned flagship of the squadron, coded 'Bravo Alpha'. My initial plan was to allocate the black-tailed 'BA' to my wingman, and take the 'markingless' XR769 for myself – it was due to be painted up as 'BB' before the end of the week, having only recently arrived from the now-defunct No. 5 Sqn. I figured that if my wingman had the black-tailed aircraft, it might make a good photograph should we all end up on the tanker with the black-tailed Phantom IIs. As it transpired, things all got too rushed and it became too difficult, so in the end I took XS901 (yet another ex-No. 5 Sqn Lightning, although it was still marked as such).

Flames lick down the fuselage as XR769 vainly struggles towards the coast.

With only minutes left before its pilot ejects, the aircraft flies on despite serious fire damage and severe scorching down its ventral tank.

Having briefed the tactics we would employ against our opponents, we walked out to the line hut and signed for our respective aircraft. Being 'air defenders', we didn't have piles of maps or other paperwork to litter the cockpit – all the information we needed was written on our small plastic kneeboards. Today, we would be simply known as 'Schubert 1' to '4', this being just one of several callsigns allocated to the last operators of the Lightning – the others were 'Rooster' and 'Eagle', which were derived from the unit's crest. Start up and the pre-take-off was rapid, and as soon as we were airborne, my wingman and I broke away from each other in classic 'Playtex' fashion. Now that we were a mile apart, we needed to start heading north out over the sea. Keeping radio silence, I began to turn, and my wingman quickly followed suit, getting back into place. We were now heading the opposite direction. With 450 knots on the ASI, I gently raised the nose of my aircraft and punched my way through airway Blue 1 at the correct height. With Lightnings' three and four now airborne, we pushed across to Boulmer radio – our usual GCI controllers – who gave us a range and bearing to the tanker. In order to stop Soviet intelligence aircraft eavesdropping on our mission progress, all sortie frequencies were coded with a three-figure number called a TAD, or fighter 'stud'. Rather than say the real frequency on the open airwaves when changing radio bands, the leader simply called a TAD number. Carried on your kneepad was a secret list that decoded all the TADs – almost a decade later, I can still remember that the initial check in was always 'TAD 026'.

We now levelled off at 25,000 ft, maintaining separation distances that allowed us to see each other visually, although not so close so as to allow a surprise attack to take all four of us out in one pass. I picked up the Victor on my radar scope at a distance of some 20 miles, and checking his height, eased the formation up to within a thousand feet of his altitude. This was done as a safety measure just in case we didn't get a visual on the tanker, and served to reduce the risk of a mid-air collision taking place. At 15 miles a sneak look outside the cockpit gave me an early 'Tally Ho'. At this range beam on, you could often visually pick the tanker up at distances beyond 20 miles. With the three Lightnings now close on my wing, I tried to make all my turns as smooth as possible, holding my speed at Mach 0.9 (around 450 knots), which gave me a 150-knot closure speed on the tanker.

Having pulled the ejection
handle, Dick Coleman departs
XR769 in copybook fashion.

At around two miles I brought the power back gently and took out the remaining height. The cockpit noise level changed as I set a lower power setting. Unlike modern aircraft, with the Lightning you hardly needed to look at the gauges as the sound and feel of the aeroplane told you what speed you were doing. Trying to touch the throttles as little as possible, and keeping the chaff-filled airbrakes firmly shut, we gently slid alongside the mighty Victor. Maintaining radio silence, I moved up alongside the cockpit, where the crew looked as if they were even more cramped than us – they nevertheless managed a cursory wave, before trailing the hoses. This told us that fuel was now available, and once the main light on the underside of the Victor went off, we were clear to approach the two hoses. Following a quick flick of the flight refuelling switch, the aerial jousting began in earnest. No sooner had we moved behind the basket when I caught sight of the F-4J(UK)s in my peripheral vision off my starboard wing. Now the pressure was on to make contact first time, and thus keep up the formation's reputation. Luckily, the air was 'smooth' at this altitude, and with a reassuring 'clunk' the probe end found its target.

Looking ahead into the refuelling pod, the various 'traffic lights' changed from amber to green to indicate fuel flow, whilst in the cockpit the multitude of lights on the control panel extinguished to show that all the tanks (ventral, flaps and wings) were quickly filling up. Just minutes after I had 'plugged in' to the drogue, it was time to disconnect. Following a gentle nudge back on the throttles, the hose began to get longer until I felt a slight pull on the aircraft and then a tug, before the basket dropped away. Sliding back close under my wingman – very close – I waited for him to finish, then with his tanks also topped off and the disconnection complete, we joined up in tight echelon. Without saying a word, we left the tanker and headed for our CAP point.

Having made sure that all the after-tanking checks had been completed, I was now left with a couple of minutes to arrange all the weapons switches in an eye-pleasing manner. Pre-attack checks completed, the Lightning was now armed and ready to fight. The sky was 'gin clear', offering optimum visibility, whilst the cold North Sea stretched out below us like a giant field of blue – it looked warm and inviting, almost like the Mediterranean. Soon our 'playmates' joined us and we set up on our standard race track. We had gone round the orbit a couple of times when our adversaries (call-sign 'Thunder') called 'fight's on' to signal that they had finished tanking and were in a position to commence the intercept. We had only one radio frequency to operate on, so we needed to keep inter-flight communication to a minimum. GCI called 'Four targets to the south, range 40, low', and with no hope of seeing them on radar, I hit the stopwatch.

Closing at around 20 miles per minute, I immediately calculated that we would merge in two minutes, and this was confirmed 60 seconds later when GCI again crackled over the radio with the call 'Range 20'. As briefed, I instructed the section to turn through 90° after the first communiqué from GCI, and then drop chaff as soon as this later distance update came in over the intercom. The flight also gained altitude whilst performing this manoeuvre so as to further confuse the enemy. Having spent some 750 hours in the back seat of a Phantom II prior to joining the Lightning fraternity, I knew that the navigators' radar pictures would have suddenly gone blank at this juncture. When in pulse-Doppler mode the AWG-10 could only detect you by tracking your forward velocity, and we had just gone to the beam, velocity zero. Having been in a similar position on numerous occasions during my Phantom II days in RAFG, I could imagine them all now realizing what had happened, and scrambling to switch their respective radars to pulse only mode. Presently, all they would see on their scopes was a mass of fluorescent blobs as our small metallic bundles of chaff fell harmlessly into the sea below. The strong wind at height dispersed the chaff over a wide area, and I made a mental note of where we had released it, as small strips of tin foil take a long time to fall 30,000 ft – it would still be around five minutes later, which in turn gave us problems as our own radar lacked a pulse-Doppler mode, and was therefore highly susceptible to chaff.

We held our beaming manoeuvre long enough to deny them a radar missile shot, but with no RWR, it was impossible to tell if we had been locked up by them. At around ten miles from the merge, GCI told us to check our height – another strictly-enforced safety measure to ensure that we were at a separate height from our opponents. The range was now down to six miles, and we were all at idle power to keep our tailpipes as cool as possible, thus avoiding the possibility of being shot down by a Sidewinder. Dead ahead I sighted a blue/grey Phantom II coming straight up at me, so I immediately put my nose on him, and in an instant we had crossed with little more than a 1,000 ft of separation. Both of us pulled

into the vertical, my radar boot having now been folded away for the duration of the combat. I looked to the left to keep him in visual contact, and I could see my wingman 10,000 ft below me also engaged with a Phantom II.

My thoughts returned to the immediate problem of how to deal with the F-4 rapidly gaining on me, and I quickly decided to reef the nose into the pure vertical and use the F.6's excess of power to climb away, safe in the knowledge that he couldn't follow me. He had bled off all his energy climbing up to my altitude on the first pass, and he was now below me out of both speed and (hopefully) ideas. My nose sliced round in response to a deft touch of rudder, and we passed each other again – closer this time, 'beak to beak'. White vapour was now streaming off his wings, which told me that he was pulling hard and losing speed. He was now fighting for his pride, not wanting to be 'shot down' by my ageing fighter. With both 'burners blazing, I eased off on the g to keep my energy up, and turned back in towards him. I could still see my wingman well below me tangled up in a similar scenario, but I could offer no assistance until I had 'disposed' of the F-4J(UK) that was again rushing headlong towards me.

Suddenly I heard a garbled 'Mayday' call on the radio, and immediately called 'Knock it off' over the radio to ask everyone to be quiet. Until we could sort this problem out the combat was over. I checked to see who had called 'Mayday' and instantly received the reply 'Schubert 2'. I was still visual with him at this point and could see a Phantom II closing in behind him, thinking he had an easy kill. I repeated the 'Stop, Stop, Stop' call and the F-4 broke away.

The Lightning was about 5,000 ft below me, trailing a white vapour from the jet pipe area, so I pulled my nose up and rolled towards him in a high g barrel roll. Still visual, I levelled out on his left-hand side, about 300 yards away, and within seconds I could fully appreciate the gravity of the situation. By now we were talking to Staxton Wold GCI, and I asked them for an immediate vector to base. At the same time I warned them to scramble the Leconfield Wessex search and rescue helicopter.

Following the ejection of a French Mirage pilot on short finals to Binbrook, a tradition was started that saw the nailing of survivors' boots to the ceiling of the officers' mess. By the end of 1988 the French lieutenant's boots had been joined by several pairs formerly belonging to Lightning pilots – the tradition explaining the presence of female underwear is less clear.

All Binbrook pilots knew that Lightnings and fires didn't mix, so it was looking highly likely that Flt Lt Coleman would have to abandon the stricken aircraft. I moved in closer to make a visual inspection of the damaged area, and saw a 20-foot flame scorching down the left side of the fuselage – the rush of air at 300 mph was fanning the flames back along the ventral tank.

We flew on in the direction of Binbrook, with GCI constantly updating us as to our position. With no sign of the fire going out, I moved in as close as I dared to get a more accurate picture of the damage, sitting just out of close formation under Dick's port wing – I dare not move any closer. Although I knew the aircraft wouldn't simply explode, the flight controls could have burned through and rolled the aircraft towards me at any moment. The damage looked bad, and from behind the missile I could see that the fuselage was open and scorched. In places I could also see sections of the ventral tank and right into the fuselage around the area of the number one engine! Cables and wires flapped in the slipstream from within the fuselage, and Dick warned me not

to get too close as his controls were now starting to stiffen up. It was now clear that this was not just a rear-end fire sadly, a not uncommon occurrence in the Lightning – as the blaze seemed to be centred around the number one engine re-heat pump.

By now we were speaking to the duty pilot at base, and Dick and I both knew what had to happen next – following signs of an unextinguished, or a positive, fire, no attempt should be made to land the aircraft. The Pilot's Notes for the Lightning stated that if the fire warning light went out and then came back on, you had to wait for a short while before checking for further signs of fire – some protection had been built into the control rods at the back of the aircraft, allowing them to withstand certain extremes of heat, but this did not guarantee that the Lightning would continue to respond to the pilot's inputs. Now that an abandonment was looking ever more likely, it was better that it be performed at a controlled height, rather than near to the ground when the aircraft may be out of control.

With only 20 miles to run to Binbrook, Dick was now down to 700 lbs of fuel in the right wing, with the left wing fuel having gone. At best, he had about seven minutes' flying time left before the engine flamed out, and we again consulted with the duty pilot back at base, who confirmed that the only option now left open to Dick was to eject. The fire one light was now on, there was no rpm indication on the number two engine. I reminded Dick to check his straps and confirm that his PSP was connected – PSP stood for personal survival pack, which contained a dinghy. This was attached to your life jacket with the aid of a fastener, and if it came undone during the ejection, you ran the risk of losing your dinghy as soon as you left the Lightning, which was not advisable when flying over the cold North Sea.

I now moved back to watch the ejection from a safe distance. By coincidence, on the previous day I had seen an aircraft having its canopy changed in the squadron hangar, and being curious as to its weight, I tried to lift it up. I failed miserably. Now well aware as to how heavy an object the canopy was, I moved well back. After what seemed like an age the canopy was blown off the Lightning and blew back over the fin. Another second passed – again it seemed like an hour – before the seat rode up the rail and Dick tumbled away from the stricken aircraft. He had ejected at 300 knots and 10,000 ft, which were the ideal operating parameters for the Martin-Baker system fitted to the F.6. I watched as Dick separated from his seat, which was quickly followed by the comforting sight of a billowing 'chute. I could see him clearly suspended beneath his multi-shaded green, white and orange canopy – coloured in such a way so as to aid detection (or evasion) when on the ground or in the water, the green being used for camouflage, whilst the orange and white were ideal location aids.

As his 'chute opened, he disappeared into a thick band of cloud, so I turned my attention to the now 'pilotless' Lightning. It began a gentle turn to the left, and as I closed in it began a shallow descent, its 'life' down to a matter of seconds. Then it seemed to level off and turn right, heading straight for the coast. Here I was behind it with nothing to shoot it down should it head inland. The aircraft looked odd devoid of its pilot, with only a large telescopic rod poking out of the cockpit where the seat had ridden up. By the time the ejection had finally taken place we were only 17 miles from the coast, and the rescue helicopter was already on its way. Like some dying beast in its final death-throes, the Lightning's nose pitched up and the fighter rolled left into a spiral descent, disappearing into cloud – at this stage I was quite close to the aircraft, and I suddenly panicked as my mind was filled with the awful vision of me descending through the same cloud only to meet XR769 coming back the other way! I quickly dismissed the thought and let down to its last known position. My visions of a re-enactment of Airplane were unfounded, as on the surface of the green murky sea was a steaming, bubbling, pool – all that remained of the F.6. After Dick's ejection the Lightning carried on flying for five-and-a-half minutes, which was probably the limit of its fuel. I could see no sign of its pilot, but my two wingmen, 'Porky' and 'Grinner', had found him, and told Binbrook that he was in his dinghy with his lifejacket inflated looking unharmed. I marked the position of the foaming grave and passed the information to Air Traffic in the unlikely event that a salvage attempt would be made, and with my fuel now getting critical, headed back to base whilst the rescue services did their job.

This incident provided me with a graphic illustration of just how good the RAF's search and rescue personnel are, for no sooner had I landed and signed the aircraft in, than my wingman arrived back at Binbrook. Apart from a small cut above his left eye caused by his helmet visor, Dick was thankfully unharmed. A decision was quickly made to leave the wreckage where it was, as the surviving Lightnings had less than a month of service left to go, and the cost of salvaging the fighter could not be justified – my photographic evidence of the aircraft taken just prior to its demise fairly accurately established the cause of the fire in any case. Lightning F.6 XR769 became the 74th, and last, Lightning to be lost in 34 years of frontline RAF service.

CHAPTER 4

Frontline

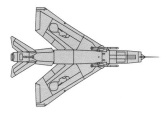

Having at last completed the seemingly endless LTF course, and feeling like the most competent fighter pilot since the likes of the Battle of Britain aces, joining your squadron quickly squashed any of your new-found illusions. It soon became apparent that during my six months at the LTF I had merely taken my first tentative steps along the long road that would eventually lead to me achieving 'operational' status. The frontline work-up comprised two distinct phases. Firstly, you were declared Limited Operational, which meant that you could hold QRA and perform any of the normal sorties, but only lead two aircraft.

Holding QRA allowed you to be vectored off into the unknown day or night, whatever the weather. Targets ranged from mighty Soviet Tu-95 Bear bombers to civilian aircraft lost, or perhaps in trouble and running short of fuel. Holding a ten-minute readiness state, whereby you had to be airborne within that time, meant that you had to have everything at your finger tips. With a maximum of one hour's fuel, you had to get the

Facing page:
Instrument Rating Training completed, the T.5 comes to a halt on runway 21. Just visible at the rear of the aircraft is the 'chute attachment to the top jet pipe area, which was anchored on with a releasable bolt.

Close to the Binbrook overhead is RAF Manby – another former World War 2 bomber base also now closed. 'BG' is seen here flying across the disused runway, inbound to Binbrook.

109

Climbing above the clouds, the formation holds echelon right at around 35,000 ft over the North Sea.

intercept right the first time, as there would be no second chance. Having successfully completed this phase, you were then trained to fully operational status. This meant that you could lead four or more aircraft, plus lead junior pilots on conversion sorties.

In traditional RAF fashion, you were not allowed to wear the official squadron cloth patch on your flying suit until you had been declared 'operational', after which it was duly presented to you by the boss. Equally prestigious was the painting of your name on the side of one of the squadron's aircraft. As a junior pilot you were normally given the first available fighter once someone had been posted away, and this gave you a vested interest in one particular aircraft, which in turn helped foster an understanding of the engineering complexities pertaining to the Lightning.

Prior to flying solo on the F.6, each new pilot flew with the squadron boss in the unit's T.5. This

allowed him to judge the calibre of the finished product provided by the LTF, as well as to gauge the competency of his new pilot. The first sortie was normally a general handling exercise, with the odd simulated emergency thrown in for good measure. After some well earned leave from the rigours of the LTF, this first trip could prove to be rather difficult following your long lay off. Like most things, flying a complex machine like the Lightning needed constant practice, and any lay off meant a slower performance. Prior to being let loose on the F.6, a check ride was flown in the simulator to cover all the different emergencies associated with the type. These focused on fuel transfer problems and overwing venting, as the rest of the systems were identical to those fitted in the F.3 – all the simulator staff had to do was 'add' more fuel to the theoretical aircraft when the pilot upgraded from 'flying' an F.3 to an F.6.

Unlike today's modern computer-driven simulators, the Lightning 'box' was amongst the first generation of all-moving, full motion, simulators. Sitting high on hydraulic jacks, it could faithfully reproduce the sensations of flight, the cockpit being painted over so as to ensure that the pilot concentrated on his instruments – there were no computer graphics on display here. As a blessing to junior pilots, the 'sim's' hydraulics were fairly unreliable, and it was often off line. The computers which drove the simulator were of a similar 1960s 'steam-driven' vintage, and took up an enormous amount of space – the ground floor of a small building, to be precise! Outside the 'box', the instructor had all the flight instruments duplicated on his console, and he could simulate any emergency with the flick of a button. Outside the 'box' was a large perspex board onto which a map of the UK had been marked out. A permanent felt-tipped pen was used to trace your flightpath onto the map, which would then prove to be a handy reference

source when debriefing the intercepts and the instrument recovery.

Having successfully completed the simulator phase, you then returned to the squadron for a brief by the unit's QFI on the handling differences of the bigger F.6 when compared with the F.3 and T.5. Prior to take-off, the mission planning now held new horizons, as no longer were you limited to performing practice diversions to the local airfields. With a seemingly abundant fuel load (at least when compared with the F.3 or T.5), the F.6 could divert to literally anywhere in the UK, or so it seemed. Depending on the weather, first solo on type was normally flown to an airfield within 20 minutes' flying time, thus allowing the novice pilot enough fuel to return to Binbrook and carry out a few circuits prior to landing. Apart from the obvious external differences associated with the enlarged and faired-in ventral tank and the gun pack, the F.6 was much the same as the F.3. On the ground it was more tail heavy, on take-off reheat was mandatory

Even if the weather was too bad for the air crew to fly, the ground crew carried on working nevertheless. The aircraft were always kept fully fuelled and, wherever possible, in a serviceable condition. As soon as the pilot cut the throttles a bowser was waiting ready to replenish the Lightning's invariably empty tanks.

and upon recovery its threshold speed was around ten knots faster due to the F.6's greater weight. In reality, the F.6 was a little easier to land than the earlier marks because its bigger wing tended to give the aircraft extra lift, and thus a cushioning effect at touchdown. Finally, with fuel in the ventral tank the g limits were slightly more restrictive, although by no means unworkable.

As it transpired, my first solo on type was – at least for the next six months – my only 'free ride' during the squadron work-up phase, each of the remaining sorties being flown with another 'operational' pilot, and assessed once back on the ground. Upon arriving, each junior pilot was assigned a 'mentor' in the form of an experienced pilot, and he was responsible for monitoring your progress and giving you assistance when it was required. I was fortunate enough to be assigned Flt Lt Steve Hunt, a former Canberra operator, and an extremely competent pilot.

With a couple of formation sorties on the F.6 behind me, the work began in earnest on the radar work-up phase. Each intercept profile was given a

code, which allowed GCI to know automatically what type of set-up you wanted in terms of target altitude and what type of control they would give you. For all latter-day Lightning pilots, the code G8D meant a 'bread and butter' intercept. The letter 'G' signified that the intercept would take place at medium level (somewhere between 10,000 and 30,000 ft), whilst the '8' meant that there would be between 90° to 180° in heading difference and the 'D' (Delta) denoted initial range information only. This letter could vary, with an 'A' (Alpha) code, for example, meaning that the intercept would have been fully controlled by GCI. The controller would give you a height to fly, headings to turn on and a speed to maintain. Hopefully this would put you two miles behind the target, ready to close for a 'kill' or 'vis-ident'. If you opted for 'B' (Bravo) control, GCI would tell you the aircraft's range and bearing every five miles until you called 'Judy', which meant that you had established contact and were happy to continue unaided. This, in essence, was how the Lightning pilot went about performing his primary peace time job.

Protecting UK airspace from intruding Soviet aircraft at all altitudes, though predominantly at medium to high level. Each peace time intercept would culminate in a visual identification of the aircraft, with the pilot recording its serial number and generally scanning the silver leviathan in search of any new modifications or additions. This, of course, was a 24-hour role, and in order to perform this task proficiently, a new pilot was 'sentenced' to a minimum of two months' 'hard labour' in the guise of the G8D in order to teach him the skills that would enable him to consistently find the target, assess its heading and make appropriate corrections, and then roll out behind it to perform the 'vis-ident', day or night.

Each day you were normally programmed to fly one or two sorties, supported by a number of sessions in the simulator for good measure. Each mission would be briefed by an experienced pilot, who would cover the 'domestic' part of the mission, followed by a detailed brief on the intercept procedures. The 'domestics' covered what radio frequencies would be used and who would be leading the take-off, performed either in close formation or stream – close formation take-offs at night were, however, not permitted. The transit to the 'play area' and the type of recovery to be flown at the end of the sortie also fell into the 'domestic' category. Throughout the brief, as a new pilot you would normally be faced with a barrage of questions concerning the weapons system, or what to do in the event of an emergency. Once into the mission itself, the experienced pilot could watch your performance from his aircraft by looking at his radar. Normally, depending on the level of recovery fuel available, you were able to perform five intercepts during a one-hour sortie. After the third intercept the leader normally gave you a break if you were coping by swapping roles for a single intercept, before he returned to being a target once again for the final 'vis-ident', prior to heading back to base.

During the debriefs on the early transformation

Most sorties involved a short transit to the 'play area' off the Lincolnshire coast, which proved to be an ideal time to take some photographs. Marc Ims is seen here piloting XS903 'BA', en route to the North Sea training area. Originally XR725 had been the OC's personal mount, but it ran out of fatigue life at the end of 1987. The second black-finned Lightning sported a larger version of the squadron's famous twin-eagle motif.

sorties all errors were covered in fine detail to ensure that the entire squadron was flying to the same standard. To help in achieving an accurate debrief on the intercepts just completed, an extremely antiquated, but nevertheless functional, arrangement was employed using two types of camera recording system fitted into the Lightning in the form of the nose-mounted G90 camera and the spine-located vis-recorder. A system also existed to record the gunsight, but this was never used during the Lightning's final months of service. The G90 was a forward-looking camera mounted in the lower bullet strut just inside the air intake, its field of view taking in the long pitot tube, which provided a handy source of reference when gauging the accuracy of the shots. The vis-recorder gave a permanent record of the radar display and weapon release. Located in the spine forward of the starter unit, it was simply a repeater of the pilot's radar scope, to the left of which was fitted an ordinary wind-up watch face, which provided a method of recording the time. To operate the recorder the pilot had to pull a switch prior to each intercept to activate the system, a

yellow light illuminated in the cockpit signifying that the film was indeed turning. Countless Lightning pilots no doubt performed the most perfect intercept ever, only to look down and find that they had inadvertently left the recorder off, and thus had no proof of their efforts.

After landing, each pilot wrote down his sortie details on a sheet, which noted his aircraft's tail number, the date and mission profile flown. This was handed to the base photographers in the line hut, who then developed the film as rapidly as possible. Often, no sooner had you finished the verbal debrief when the film was ready to be scrutinized by the squadron weapons officer. Located in a blacked-out room in the No. 11 Sqn building was an ancient projector that would have been more at home showing Charlie Chaplin films in the 1920s than air defence sorties of the 1980s. Each intercept was analysed in detail, and any errors in technique highlighted for correction on subsequent sorties. After a week of day flying, the new pilot was given a night dual check either with the squadron QFI or QWI. This was also a chance for the latter to

No. 11 Sqn's last Lightning photo call in April 1988. The pilots are, from left to right, Ian 'Doof' McDonald-Webb, Marc 'Gibbon' Ims, Dick Coleman (RAAF), John 'J C' Carter, Simon Braithwaite, Chris 'B P' Berners-Price, Wg Cdr Jake Jarron (the boss), Derek 'Grinner' Smith, Ian 'Bucket' Hollingworth, Steve 'Alf' Moir, Paul Cooper, John 'B J' Aldington, Paul Sutton, Alan 'Porky' Page, the Author and Mike Baird (the unit's junior Engineering Officer).

The main reason why XR725 didn't last until the end of Lightning operations can be traced to the extensive phase of air combat it undertook in late 1987. Photographed from a No. 79 Sqn Hawk, 'BA' heads out over the sea for yet another two v two dissimilar air combat sortie.

check your competency at performing 'vis-idents' at night. Having passed this strenuous hurdle, you were now cleared to undertake intercepts day and night with 'vis-idents' on targets with lights on.

All this training was building up to the phase three 'vis-ident' check ride. Like the intercepts, Lightning 'vis-idents' were coded, with a phase one denoting a sortie against a target in daylight, a phase two on a target at night with its lights on and not in cloud, and a phase three on a contact either at night with its lights off or in cloud by day. This permitted you to join onto a tanker even if he was in cloud, using your radar to obtain visual contact with him. Occasionally, it was the only option if the cloud was solid from sea level to 40,000 ft, whilst in wartime it was more tactical to hide the tanker in cloud.

Two 11 Sqn F6s refuel from a 101 Sqn VC10 tanker with a third two-seat Lightning from 5 Sqn. The VC10 tanker was a relative newcomer to the Lightning force, the majority of contacts being made with the venerable Victor Mks 1 and 2.

Sadly, when I first started taking the photographs for this book in 1986 Fuji hadn't yet invented Velvia slide film, which is particularly suited to air-to-air photography. Happily, by 1992 it was available, and as this shot illustrates, its richness of colour is unequalled.

At this stage in the conversion the *ab initio* pilot was of little use to the squadron, as he was unable to take part in exercises or air-to-air refuelling missions. Prior to any major exercise taking place, non-operational pilots were normally assigned to other training courses to keep them occupied such as a visit to a GCI site, or the completion of the air-to-air refuelling syllabus. You could even be sent away to one of the RAF's Flying Training Schools (FTSs) to complete your annual spinning ride. Although the Lightning could recover from a spin, intentional spinning was prohibited. A spin in a Lightning was a fairly violent affair, and often resulted in a bent pitot probe. Unnecessary aircraft damage, coupled with the fact that the height loss in a Lightning could be as much as 20,000 ft a minute in a spin with the nose 60° below the horizon, meant that pilots had to go off-base to an FTS to achieve the appropriate rating in the logbook. Fortunately for Binbrook pilots, the Jet Provost had similar spin recovery drills, and was therefore used in place of the vastly more expensive Lightning. The Lightning pilot in the right-hand seat called out the spin recovery drill for the Lightning whilst the instructor tried to recover

the aeroplane by implementing your instructions.

You were usually allowed to fly the humble 'JP' back to base after the spinning had been completed to make you realize just how awesome the Lightning really was. The trainer seemed so small and fragile when compared with the Lightning, and often the instructor became alarmed as you flew round the final turn in the light buffet, which was perfectly acceptable in the Lightning but not a good idea in the Jet Provost.

If any single aspect of flying the Lightning could be regarded as an everyday event, it had to be air-to-air refuelling. Prior to undertaking this phase of the operational work-up, each pilot spent a couple of days at Marham (now at Brize Norton) learning the mechanics of refuelling whilst travelling at 300 m.p.h. at 30,000 ft. Detailed briefings were given on the refuelling pods, delivery rates and emergency procedures, and films were shown illustrating how to refuel off all the current tanker types.

In the past the Lightning had refuelled from the Valiant, Sea Vixen and Vulcan, but in its final years of service the VC10, Victor and Buccaneer were its only regular sources of supply. In times of crisis

plans and trials were carried out using USAF KC-135s, but these were rarely used on a daily basis. The American system slightly differs from that used by the RAF in that as soon as you make contact with the drogue you move to the left or right, thus forming a loop with the hose – a tricky procedure that has a high chance of causing a whiplash which would snap the end of your probe tip off. Having attended the course you were now ready to have a go on your own.

As the shape of the T.5 forward fuselage varied markedly from the single-seater, its refuelling characteristics were also different. Therefore, your first sortie was flown solo in a F.6, in company with an experienced leader who sat alongside you in another aircraft giving advice. In the cockpit there was very little involved – you simply flicked on a switch on the instrument panel prior to contact, which duly illuminated a row of lights to show you into which tank the fuel was going. Normal procedure was for the leader to perform the join, with the wingman staying reasonably close behind. Prior to each sortie you were told on which tanker tow line your Victor or VC10 would be situated, these dedicated areas being sited mostly over the North Sea where the tankers orbit, giving fighter pilots a rough idea of where to look and where to head. In the days before the Gulf War and other

international crises, the RAF had an abundance of tankers, and it was often easy to 'bootleg' slots at short notice. However, due to so many overseas commitments, all that has changed.

On normal day-to-day missions, GCI would often tell you whilst airborne that a tanker was available nearby with fuel to spare, and as mission leader all you had to do was contact squadron operations over the radio and ask if you were cleared to tank. Normally the response was in the affirmative, as long as there were no other commitments that required you back at Binbrook in a hurry. On one occasion near the end of 1987, a pair of Lightnings were airborne for six hours after refuelling five times – they had originally planned for a one-hour mission! A great plus point of the Lightning was its enormous thrust, which meant that refuelling at almost any height was possible, with the laid down limit being 43,000 ft. For a new pilot arriving alongside the tanker for the first time, the sight of a bigger aircraft in close formation was a memorable one. With the wing hoses trailed, each fighter moved behind their respective baskets, awaiting clearance to make contact. After the first Lightning had plugged in, it was then your turn to try and 'hit' the basket – an exercise which has been described as 'trying to take a rolling jump at a running basket'. Experience soon taught you that all that was needed

There was nothing in the book to say that you couldn't tank with the gear down, but on the other hand there was nothing which said that you could! The undercarriage limiting speed was 250 knots, which coincided with the minimum tanking speed. With the gear down, fuel consumption increased dramatically and, as already stated, your max speed was limited to 250 knots. One anonymous pilot thought he would give his wingman a particularly difficult slow-speed target to identify way out over the North Sea, but little did he realize the problems he was about to unleash on himself. Selecting gear down, he reduced speed to around 170 knots in order to simulate a civilian aircraft lost outside normal air traffic cover. The junior wingman dutifully completed his intercept and came alongside the leader to offer all the necessary assistance to a civilian in distress that regulations required. Once the leader had decided that the exercise was complete, he ordered that the pair return to base. After his first selection of gear up proved fruitless, he was left with a real dilemma. It was over 100 miles to the nearest base, and with his fuel consumption now three times its normal rate, he was going to fall short by a long way. Luckily, after a few applications of positive and negative g the problem cleared itself, and the gear came back up.

APC detachment over, four
Lightning pilots prepare to
return to UK.

was to pick a reference point in the cockpit like the
standby compass, and run this up a dayglo line on
the tanker – all refuellers have such markings
painted underneath the wing to help you achieve the
correct line. The Lightning probe was fitted on the
left wing out of sight, so it wasn't really possible to
try and visually guide it into the basket, particularly
on the early sorties.

Many Lightning legends have evolved around
tanking missions, one of the most famous
concerning the F.6 pilot who, in customary fashion,
announced that he was short of fuel and would like
to 'plug' (make contact) straight away. His low fuel
state became clear when the tanker transferred more
than the F.6's total maximum uplift! Other tales
concerned the early days when some aircraft lacked
probes, one explaining how an embarrassed senior
officer returned to base short of fuel, having
discovered whilst alongside the tanker that his
aeroplane wasn't fitted with a probe!

After several visits to the tanker, the task became

much simpler, although refuelling in turbulence
could be tricky – with the basket bouncing up and
down several feet, it becomes very difficult to make
contact. Having achieved day and night proficiency
on the basket, the last sortie in this phase comprised
a cross-country mission with a tanker, ending back
at Binbrook for an accompanied letdown. The
whole procedure was designed to give the novice
pilot experience in deploying with a Victor or VC10
to some far off overseas base.

Standard procedure meant that if the Lightning
had an emergency en route, the tanker would lead
the diversion, freeing the single-seat pilot of the
workload associated with the radios and navigation,
and thus leaving him to concentrate on dealing with
the problem. The tanker's multi-crew and
sophisticated navigation suite seemed perfectly
suited to carrying out this task, but in reality this
was often not the case. Tanker crews usually operate
alone, so the role of formation leader is alien to
them, and often results in fraught moments for

fighter pilots! I have vivid memories of my own particular cross-country – a two-hour-and-fifty-minute mission alongside a Victor and a fellow No. 11 Sqn Lightning. The weather was fortunately 'gin clear', and with the sortie having gone as planned, it was decided to initiate a recovery to Binbrook alongside the tanker. Each Lightning took up his place, one on each wing tip in vic formation on the Victor. All was going according well until a short distance from the runway when the Victor pilot lowered his undercarriage. Due to the massive amount of drag caused when the wheels came down, there was no way the two Lightnings could stay in formation even at idle power with full airbrake. We were now in the unusual formation of reverse vic, with two Lightnings ahead and the huge tanker quite low down at fairly low speed. In the end it was every man for himself, and we all overshot and turned away, with the Victor flying directly ahead!

Although not strictly part of the work-up, air-to-air gunnery was nevertheless an essential part of a Lightning pilot's skills. Normally, both Nos 5 and 11 Sqns deployed to Cyprus – where they were guaranteed better weather and uncongested airspace – for air-to-air firing camps, each unit detaching back-to-back, thereby sharing air transport and

allowing certain rectification equipment to be left in situ. When the LTF was still in operation, each squadron would take half of the staff pilots out with them to allow them to keep current on the gun-armed F.6.

Only British designers could have placed a cannon directly in front of a fuel tank, but in their defence, it never caused any problems. The gun pack toted two electrically-fired and controlled 30 mm Aden guns, each weapon being made for either a left- or right-hand feed, which in turn precluded them from being interchangeable. Around six feet long, each gun weighed 192 lbs, and was capable of firing 1,200 to 1,400 rounds per minute, or one six-second trigger burst. On the ground, the guns were made safe by the insertion of the armament safety key, located in the starboard wheel well and instantly visible with its red and white flag hanging down. Each Aden could carry a maximum of 120 rounds, and all spent cases were kept in compartments behind the guns.

Prior to deploying on Armament Practice Camp (APC), all pilots that had not fired guns in the past year performed a dual ride with the squadron weapons officer over the North Sea prior to transiting to Cyprus. As the T.5 had no guns, all

Just as the old Lightning pilot expression stated that 'one peep was worth a thousand sweeps', this picture speaks a thousand words. XR725 sits on the Akrotiri flightline surrounded by the paraphernalia associated with air-to-air gunnery. On the left is a trolley crammed with painted ammunition primed for loading, whilst on the trolley to the right are loaded gun cases ready for fitting. In between the two trolleys is the brake parachute, which was normally fitted below the lower jet pipe. On top of the parachute is the strong steel cabling which wrapped around the rear part of the jet pipes.

Loading the Lightning. The gun bay doors are open beneath the ventral tank as the ground crew replenish the empty ammunition boxes. The size of the shell cases and the warhead are easily visible in this shot.

attacks comprised ciné runs on the banner target, with the instructor in the right-hand seat trying to give advice as best as possible for he had no gun sight! As well as possessing excellent weather, Cyprus also allowed the squadron to practice its secondary role of overseas reinforcement.

The deployment itself was a fairly momentous event, as trying to send ten ageing aeroplanes several thousand miles all on the same day required its fair share of engineering miracles to take place. In the late 1970s and early 1980s, the Lightnings had deployed to Cyprus by staging through France, Italy and Greece, but the complications involved were so great that tanking soon became the preferred option. A week before deployment day, the squadron T.5 was despatched to Marham to brief the route with the Victor crew, as well as checking a plethora of details like fuel uplift, tanking brackets, suitable diversions en route and radio procedures. Finally, the topic of in-flight emergencies was covered in detail so that all eventualities were catered for.

On the day of deployment all the engineers would be in at dawn preparing the Lightnings for an early start, thus allowing the aircraft to land at a reasonable hour in Cyprus, bearing in mind the time difference. Often the weather in the UK would delay the take-off, or an unserviceability with the tankers might affect the departure time, but when the go ahead was finally given, all the Lightnings would usually get airborne in groups of three or four, with the T.5 bringing up the rear. Additional aircraft normally flown by the other squadron pilots, or the LTF, would also take-off as airborne spares should anyone have a technical problem and have to return. These replacement Lightnings would normally go as far as the UK boundary, and then providing all was okay, turn back. Otherwise, it was a case of replacing the unserviceable aircraft, resulting in a few days of unplanned sunshine in Cyprus. With its meagre fuel load, the T.5 was the worst aircraft to have to deploy in, as it required up to ten refuelling contacts to reach Cyprus – in fact at some points in the transit you were obliged to remain 'plugged in', as you were out of range of any suitable diversions! The T.5 was taken to keep pilots current on all the various check rides needed during the six-week stay.

Having successfully arrived in Cyprus, all the aircraft had their missiles removed and the guns prepared for firing. The Lightning was no stranger to RAF Akrotiri, as the F.6s of No. 56 Sqn had been the last permanently-based fighters on the island, and traces of their existence still remained over a decade after their return to the UK.

The aim of every pilot in Cyprus was to become 'Ace' qualified at air-to-air shooting, this qualification being an annual NATO requirement for air defence pilots. To achieve this you had to place 15 per cent of your bullets on target *twice* during a maximum of six sorties. If you failed to attain this score, you had to start all over again from square one. Outside the operations room stood a large board onto which was written all the pilots' individual scores, which were updated on a daily basis. With air-to-air shooting, there is no way of verbally winning the debrief, as the results are there for all to see on the flag.

The targets were towed by Canberras of No. 100 Sqn, based at Wyton, who maintained an almost permanent detachment in Cyprus providing a service for all the RAF's air defence squadrons. The target itself was a white six-foot by thirty-foot banner made of woven hessian, which was towed 300 yards behind the Canberra. At one end of the banner was the spreader bar, a large fibre-glass tube inside which were housed radar reflectors. At each end of the tube were two heavy metal discs which allowed the banner to roll smoothly down the runway. The whole assembly was towed on a long length of nylon strop, attached to the banner by six cords.

Getting the banner airborne was a tricky procedure, as it had to be laid beside the Canberra on the edge of the runway. As the Canberra, or 'Tug', rolled down the runway, the banner was dragged into the sky, whereupon Air Traffic would call 'Flag normal'. If at any stage the banner became twisted or broken, the pilot of the 'Tug' had to immediately jettison it. Towing the flag made the Canberra single-engine critical just at the moment of take-off, so the whole procedure had to be handled delicately from a pilot's point of view. Once airborne, the 'Tug' would head south over the Mediterranean to the live firing range, which was situated some 25 miles off the coast. This could take some time as the cloth banner was limited to a maximum speed of 200 knots – any faster and the slipstream would start to fray the back end of the flag, which was an alarming state of affairs if all your hard earned hits were at the back of the banner!

Only once the Canberra was safely airborne would the first two Lightning pilots prepare to start their engines – it was no problem to strap into the cockpit and then be airborne five minutes later. Once aloft, the most important thing to get out of the way was trimming the aircraft for 350 knots – the ideal firing speed. It was possible to set the aircraft up then disconnect the trimmer so that you couldn't subconsciously re-trim it later in flight. Up on Mount Olympus, the GCI would give you a

THE AKROTIRI HILTON

The last time both Lightning squadrons were all together was at Akrotiri in mid-1987 – No. 5 Sqn below and No. 11 Sqn above.

vector to steer to try and find the 'Tug', and from here on in the pressure was on. Flying together as a pair in a 'fighting wing' configuration or a couple of spans out from close formation, the lead pilot set up for the first attack.

Once at 8,000 ft, the Canberra pilot began flying a figure eight pattern, consisting of a 180° turn to the right, followed by a straight leg, then a 180° turn to the left, followed by a straight leg. Trying to keep a datum heading of say north, the 'Tug' pilot would keep calling his heading so that the two Lightnings could correct their patterns. Once the 'Tug' called

'steady on heading', the lead Lightning pilot aimed to be 2,800 yards behind the banner. At this point the leader called 'commence', and the 'Tug' went into his pattern. The 'one-armed paper hanger' routine now began in earnest in the cockpit. The pilot selected 'gunsight on', folded the radar 'boot' away and switched the transmitter off, prior to ensuring that 'Guns' were selected. On the early sorties all passes were made with the camera, so a second call of 'in ciné' was made, to which the tug replied 'clear ciné'. This was a safety requirement – obviously, if he could see a boat below and the pilot called 'in hot' (guns), then the tug would reply 'ciné only'. Now came the tricky part.

As the Lightning lacked radar-ranging, it was all a question of judgement in order to arrive at the correct bracket. It was actually possible to lock the radar to the banner and use radar-ranging, but this was seldom employed. In theory, the radar locked to the target at a range of between 1,350 and 500 ft, and a light illuminated to the right of the gunsight to show that you were in range for a shot. However, as the correct bracket was actually between 400 and 350 yards, it was deemed more accurate to estimate the range.

Having tipped in on the flag, the most important thing was to achieve the correct line so that your flightpath was moving in the same sense as the banner. After a while you knew if you had achieved the correct line as your wing tip would touch the flag's slipstream, and you would in turn feel a very slight burble through the controls. At long range it was a piece of cake to track the pipper on the banner. However, as the range closed it became increasingly more difficult as the g built up, along with the angle of bank and the rate of closure. At 1,000 yards the small circle in the centre of the gunsight should have been the same width as the banner, signalling that it was time to start tracking it. Once down to 500 yards you smoothly brought the pipper up to the front of the banner, paused until it passed through 400 yards, then fired, followed by a swift 'breakout' away from the target. All this happened in a couple of seconds, the secret being to have the cadence of 'same, half, pause and FIRE' etched onto your memory cells.

The ideal firing picture was 350 yards and 350 knots at 16° angle off. The angle off was very important, as below about five degrees you were looking straight up the flag at the back end of the Canberra. At this angle you ran the very real risk of hitting the 'Tug', so a ten-degree limit was imposed. If the angle off was greater than 25° it became more difficult to track the banner. Breaking out, you made the trigger 'safe' and called 'out', before repeating the whole gunnery procedure once again – the wingman tipping in just after the leader. Having

made six or seven passes, it was time to let the formation behind you go onto the flag whilst you returned to Akrotiri.

Once back in the line hut, you then had to try and remember how many passes you had made on the banner, whether they were left- or right-hand turns, and if you had made any errors, before explaining all this to the squadron weapons officer (known as the IWI) during the film debrief. IWIs were generally fairly hard task masters, with 'death by ciné film' being no exaggeration. Each frame could be analysed in minute detail with 'Heath Robinson' assessment charts made from scraps of graph paper, which were used to calculate range at trigger press and angle off. As a junior pilot, you were normally detailed as the IWI's personal secretary, and I had the pleasure of watching about three miles worth of ciné film in two weeks – actually no bad thing, as I then knew all the common errors before making them myself! Once the IWI was happy that you were safe and accurate, you were cleared 'hot' and the scores were now available for all to view.

Prior to flying your first 'live' sortie, you had to check in with the ops room to ascertain both the range slot time and the callsign of your target. Next door you could see which colour of rounds had been loaded into your aircraft, as well as the quantity. Each Lightning was loaded with bullets whose tips were dipped in different-coloured paint, which meant that when they hit the banner they left a coloured mark which could then be identified as your hit – an old system, but nevertheless an effective one. If your aircraft went unserviceable and you took a spare, you had to then make sure that no one else was firing the same colour as you, as with up to six aircraft firing on one banner during a single sortie, this could pose identification problems. Normally we fired red, blue, green, yellow, brown and purple tipped shells, although for some reason most pilots preferred to shoot red – probably because it was easier to see any hits when you checked the banner after the last pass.

On my first live shoot I fell for an old trick that with my previous experience as a navigator I should have been wise to. On my second pass I arrived

somewhere near the right picture and squeezed the trigger, and to my horror the top of the spreader bar flew off and then the banner became detached from its strop and fell 8,000 ft into the sea! I'd shot the banner clean off on my first pass – a rare event. As the mission was abruptly cancelled, I came back to the Akrotiri overhead and burnt off some fuel doing aerobatics whilst the Canberra, minus banner, landed. Shortly afterwards I touched down and taxied back to the dispersal, not duly concerned about the proceedings of the curtailed sortie. I signed the aeroplane back in and walked to the ops room, but I never actually got my foot in the door as I was physically grabbed by the squadron IWI and taken around the side of the building. In front of me lay a length of nylon strop about 20 ft long with an unmistakable red slash the same colour as my bullets on the split end. The other end held the mounting buckle normally attached to the Canberra.

My heart sank as I realized the seriousness of what I'd done – I had come within 20 ft of getting the one and only Lightning air-to-air kill. I was mortified. I racked my brains as to what I'd done wrong, whilst the IWI questioned me about my parentage, and told me that I had better go and see the Canberra crew and apologize to them. Visions of a bar bill the size of Mount Olympus flashed through my head as I walked back into the ops room where, instead of glum faces, I was confronted by a group of giggling Lightning pilots and an equally amused Canberra crew. Confused as to why they thought the incident so funny, I was let into the ruse.

Whilst I had been burning off fuel in the overhead, the squadron had got what was left of an old strop, cut it into a suitable 20-ft length and daubed the end liberally with red paint. I had fallen hook, line and sinker for the jape, and was more than a little relieved to see my film, which confirmed that the flag was shot off just next to the spreader bar.

As mentioned earlier, fellow Lightning pilot Flt Lt 'Charlie' Chan was less fortunate than I when under a month later during the No. 5 Sqn APC, his newly-modified F.6 XR763 ingested a six-inch metal wheel shot off on a firing pass. The aircraft managed to remain in the air until just short of Akrotiri, when it lost power and Chan was forced to eject – fortunately he sustained few injuries.

As the APC progressed the squadron scoreboard gradually filled up, and as each pilot became 'Ace' qualified, a small black ace appeared by their name. Once each pilot was duly qualified, he moved onto limited operational firing, which meant that he had a certain number of bullets to fire on a given number of passes, thus keeping the pressure on. This culminated in the 'op' shoot, 'op' standing for operational. Now the aim was to get just one hit on the banner.

For training the Lightning used practice ammunition – an inert 30 mm round about eight inches long and weighing 1 lb. The case was made of brass, which contained the propellant, onto which was fitted the projectile. Around the projectile was a copper driving band. Several different types of warhead could be fitted, the most lethal being HE (high explosive). It was calculated that one round of HE fired in the right place would probably bring an aircraft down.

Although the academic pattern had seemed rushed, nothing prepared you for the hurricane speed of the 'op' pattern. With only 40 rounds loaded, you had just two passes to get one bullet on the banner. Unlike on previous runs, you now met the Canberra head on, with a combined closing speed of 600 knots, aiming to pass as close as you dared, but not inside 500 ft. As you searched for the target on the radar, one eye was looking out front to try and get an early 'tally ho' on the Canberra. Once this had been achieved, the radar 'boot' could be folded away, and you gingerly pointed the aircraft towards the target, aiming to give the 'Tug' as close a 'dust off' as you dared. The crux of this mission was to be calling 'commence' exactly as you passed abeam of the Canberra, but trying to judge exactly when this would occur could be a bit difficult. Most pilots tended to start the call early, pronouncing the word 'commence' in a rather elasticised fashion, as the final letter was the executive command for the 'Tug' to start turning. As the Canberra turned

Not since World War 2 has one single aircraft generated so much national pride – the Lightning was thoroughly British.

towards you, you would thrash the stick in his direction, reefing the Lightning into a cruelly tight turn. Your g-suit inflated, squeezing hard around your legs, thus letting your senses know that your were pulling around 5 g without a reference to the accelerometer. A hard turn through 90° and your head swivelled round, trying desperately to keep a tally on the flag. If you lost sight of it at this point, any chances of firing had just gone out the window.

The highly swept wing started to buffet, which signalled that it was time to kick the 'burners in order to peg the speed at 350 knots. Now you were visual with the banner, and in the few seconds prior to squeezing the trigger you were obliged to sort the

speed out, get the right height and establish your line – '1000 yards half, 400 yards same, pause, add "one potato" as it's an "op" shoot, and "Fire", trigger safe and "break out"'. The Canberra pilot then told you how far he'd turned, and you repositioned for a last pass. This time you could squeeze the trigger a tad longer to 'fire out' the ammunition, as there was no point in taking the bullets back home.

The 'op' shoot was tremendous fun, but a very demanding profile to fly. Sometimes pilots got so disorientated that they ended up attacking the banner from the opposite side that they started from! Despite the heavy workload, the sortie at least gave you a chance to handle the Lightning in a real

LAST OF THE LIGHTNINGS

combat-type scenario, with none of the modern high-tech 'gizmos' available to today's pilots there to help you. It is true to say that the banner was never peppered with bullet holes, the average being around 17 per cent, but then it was all done on 'gut feeling' and pilot skill, which is what made it so challenging.

With the 'op' shoots over, the last event of the APC was, time permitting, the 'inter-Flight' shoot. If there were enough bullets left over, a competition was held between the two flights – 'A' and 'B'. Each flight commander picked his four best air-to-air pilots, and each was allocated an aircraft. The four Lightnings each had a full load of 240 rounds, decorated with a multitude of colours which served to preserve the anonymity of those who shot. Both flights had their own banner to shoot at, which was marked by the impartial squadron IWI. To further add a 'touch of spice' to the proceedings, each team

was also marked for the best departure and arrival from Akrotiri. The stakes were high, as the losing flight had to buy the winners' after-dinner drinks at the end-of-detachment dinner. These usually comprised the lethal No. 11 Sqn cocktail, appropriately coloured black and yellow thanks to a mix of coffee liqueur and advocat.

On the very last inter-flight shoot it was decided to give the squadron commander's collection of 1960s 'kipper' ties a true Viking burial – some seven ties were duly sown onto a banner and fired at by one of the flights. Only one survived this ordeal unscathed.

With the shooting over, the final act was to fly all the squadron's aircraft in a 'Diamond Nine' formation. Normally, the two-seater would act as both an airborne spare and whip for these sorties, the latter job seeing its pilot literally 'whipping' the

My forward fuselage casts a shadow across the fin of 'BN', immersed in the golden orange light of dusk.

This photograph could have been taken in the early 1960s, but was actually shot some 30 years later.

formation into place so that the whole thing looked symmetrical. Unfortunately, for the last No. 11 Sqn 'Diamond Nine', the flagship 'BA' was unavailable due to engine problems, but a memorable flypast was performed nevertheless, with the T.5 acting as whip, spare, photo-chase and number nine in the formation! Having taken off in a ten-second stream, followed by a standard rotation climb, the whole affair was over as the sun set 30 minutes later.

By 24 June 1987 the Lightnings of our sister-squadron had arrived, and it was time for the unit to make its final departure from the island. After five hours and twenty minutes airborne – and more refuelling contacts than I care to remember – all the squadron Lightnings were safely back in the cold, grey, skies of Lincolnshire. With the fun flying over, it was back to the serious work of completing my limited combat ready work-up phase. Despite the aircraft having less than a year to run in frontline service, standards were maintained until the end on the Lightning force. The future for the airfield,

however, looked bleak, as with little or no modernization having taken place in the decades since World War 2, it too was due for closure. The final, irrevocable, countdown had begun.

With the carefree visual flying of the APC now just a distant memory, I started training for some of the most demanding intercepts performed by the Lightning force. Still to come were supersonic intercepts, 'high flyers' and low-level fast targets. Increasingly now the targets were evading more and more, making the job that much harder. For a variety of reasons supersonic attacks were difficult, the most obvious being the sheer speed at which things happened. People talk of both time compression and the elasticity of time, depending on the circumstances. When two machines are closing at 30 miles a minute five miles above the North Sea at night, and you're alone in a small metal box strapped to an aluminium rocket, you soon understand the meaning of time compression.

One Lightning pilot almost paid the ultimate price

for what was a lapse in concentration that lasted little more than a few seconds. He became disorientated at night in cloud whilst chasing another Lightning, and suddenly his peaceful world changed to one of sheer panic. Fixated by the radar for too long, when he looked back at his instruments he found himself nearly vertical at Mach 1.3 at around 17,000 ft, and heading down! Selecting idle, he knew an attempt at ejection would be futile, so he pulled hard back on the stick and hoped for the best. As the aircraft went subsonic the g increased and he blacked out. When he came around the Lightning was climbing through 6,000 ft. The aircraft pulled in excess of 10g, and had come within 250 ft of hitting the sea – a remarkable escape. The aircraft – XS898 – was repaired and served right to the end of the Lightning era.

The supersonic attack could only be performed with Red Top missiles fitted due to their limited head on capability – 'limited' was probably an understatement, as the target had to be travelling at speeds in excess of Mach 1.5 to generate enough skin friction heat to attract the weapon's infrared seeker head. Despite this major operational drawback, the biggest limitation imposed on the supersonic intercept profile centred not on the weapon's short comings, but rather the Lightning's fuel consumption. More than ever, fuel checks

Looking more like a brass rubbing than an aircraft, XR773 basks in a rare winter sunset.

From a pilot's point of view, the Lightning always gave you a feeling of confidence. As long as you didn't let the speed drop, there was little you couldn't do in the aircraft. 'AD' is seen here performing a slow roll at around 40,000 ft.

became second nature at supersonic speeds, as travelling at Mach 1.6, you could cover 90 miles in five minutes – resulting in potentially grave consequences if you were heading away from the coast. Suddenly, you were checking your position every few minutes, and with the Lightning's limited navigational aids, you had to cross-check with GCI, who would keep you informed of your 'pigeons' (your range and bearing) back to base.

Also of paramount importance on these sorties was to keep ahead of the ever-changing weather back at Binbrook. Flying 100 miles out over the North Sea, the meteorological conditions could be very different from the Lincolnshire wolds. With a deteriorating weather pattern back at Binbrook, you could quickly go from having enough fuel for another intercept to being below the diversion limit, and rapidly running out of ideas.

As soon as GCI told you your target was 'high speed', it was fair enough to consider him hostile. In wartime, no one was likely to be flying towards the UK coast at 18 miles per minute with friendly intentions! This immediately ruled out the need to

identify the target, and with little room in the cramped cockpit for storing operational manuals, all your intercept profiles had to be memorized off by heart. Now was not the time to be reaching for a file to see when to start the acceleration profile – if you missed the intercept first time around, a re-attack was not really an option against a target doing Mach 1.6. This was a one shot deal.

Supersonically, the Lightning performed best at Mach 1.3 – a speed it could maintain in a fairly hard turn. It also gave you the chance to perform a stern conversion if required. At long range GCI would give you a range and bearing to the target, and all your initial turns were based on this information. At 40 miles, as long as you had reached the magic Mach 1.3, it was time to climb and take out some of the height. The AI.23 radar did have some computer modes to help you with the attack, giving you information when to turn and climb to put you in the best firing bracket. A constant check was needed as you climbed, looking deep the six o'clock for any signs of contrailing. Then as it is today, leaving a huge white line across the sky advertising your presence is tactically unsound.

With the two fighters rushing towards each other at a combined speed of 30 miles per minute, events took place in rapid time. At 30 miles a cursory glance was made at the weapons panel to check that the missiles were armed, before selecting the target's speed on the computer. Bearing in mind that the maximum range you were going to detect the target on radar was 23 miles, this preparation gave you about 30 seconds to get a lock and sort out the geometry. As soon as you had a contact you moved the acquisition, or lock circle, to a point at 15 miles on the radar. Making sure you were painting him accurately in the middle of the beam, you raised the scanner one or two degrees to allow for the fact that he was coming towards you at a higher altitude. With a bit of luck he would then literally fly into the beam, thus giving you just enough time to squeeze the acquisition trigger and lock him up.

As soon as the radar was tracking the target the picture changed, displaying a steering dot inside a circle. This dot gave you the commands to either

climb, descend or fly left or right. When the launch warning light came on the trigger was squeezed, and automatically at around six miles the missile left the rail. The launch range was a function of target speed, as a faster target could be engaged at up to ten miles. At six miles from the target when flying on a collision course, the missile would travel for around 12 seconds before impact. The quickest way to stop your climb and avoid any collision was to roll the aeroplane onto its back and pull. When you got too close to the target a breakaway warning cross appeared on the screen to prompt you to disengage if, for some reason, you had (as sometimes happened) suffered a momentary brain failure.

To re-attack the target was an equally difficult task, bearing in mind he had just crossed you on an opposite heading doing Mach 1.6. Your task was to try and get two miles behind him and keep your speed from going subsonic. At roll out ranges in excess of five miles, either you ran out of fuel or airspace before you caught him up. It was whilst performing a re-attack that the pilot was most likely to lose control of the aircraft. Trying to re-acquire him with your head in the radar and the aircraft in full reheat, whilst pulling as tight a turn as possible, often saw the Lightning bleed off all its energy and then inform you of your error with a transonic pitch up.

Intercepting a high flying target was very similar in many respects to performing a supersonic attack, and again was very much a Lightning speciality. Like a supersonic intercept, a long time was spent in reheat when flying this attack profile, so fuel awareness was still paramount. In peacetime, the single-seat Lightning was limited to an upper height of 50,000 ft, whilst the two-seater was limited to 43,000 ft. In reality, everyone knew that the aircraft would go much, much, higher than this, and pilots

With so many aircraft available for the engineers to rob parts from, it was inevitable that some panels would get swapped around as aircraft were withdrawn. Here, XS903 seems to have gained a few panels from a time-expired aircraft. The back end of the Lightnings were normally shiny due to all the oil that spilled over when the engines were up and running.

The very last Lightning 'Diamond Nine' ever put up shows the variety of different colours that had been adopted throughout the fleet by the time the aircraft was retired.

Facing page:
The daily scene in the No. 11 Sqn hangar. Surrounded by servicing equipment, a trio of Lightnings undergo maintenance.

who flew the Lightning in its early years were often photographed wearing Taylor helmets and full pressure suits. These bulky spaceman-like assemblies had long since been discarded by the time I arrived at Binbrook, and the limit of 50,000 ft was strictly adhered to.

All Lightning pilots attended a short course at RAF North Luffenham, home of the aviation medicine department of the RAF, prior to being sent to the LTF. Here, all potential operators were subjected to pressure breathing – a most unpleasant and unnatural experience – which was enough to convince you to stick to altitudes below 50,000 ft.

The suggested technique for climbing the Lightning above ceilings of 45,000 ft was to put the aircraft into a 30° climb at supersonic speed. This angle would clearly take you rapidly up to 60,000 ft, so a slightly less-dramatic angle was adopted. The rarefied atmosphere above 40,000 ft potentially posed engine and/or reheat problems for the pilot.

Having a double 'flame out', with the associated rapid decompression, was an emergency not to be taken lightly.

Very often the Lightning would be tasked to intercept and identify high flying targets, the USAF's U-2s often being a favourite choice. Stories exist of pilots in the 1960s sailing past U-2s flying at heights approaching 65,000 ft, much to the amazement of the American pilots – whether or not the Lightning pilot was completely in control of his mount at this altitude is open to debate!

On 22 August 1987 the public got its last chance to see the RAF's most enigmatic fighter at close hand. Billed as the 'Last, Last Lightning Show', the event was to be highlighted by an 11-ship flypast which would open the day's flying programme. At the eleventh hour, the typically dank British summer weather that had plagued Lincolnshire all day, lifted just long enough for the Lightnings to get airborne. This was a great moment for all the station's

'Kit form' Lightning XS925 is prepared for its trip down the A1 to the RAF Museum at Hendon. The nose has already been removed and the centre wing-box section has been split.

engineers, who had worked so hard to get so many aircraft serviceable.

For a long time all major servicing of the Lightning had taken place at Binbrook, the RAF logically deciding as all remaining Lightnings were based there, it would make more sense to establish a facility on-site – therefore, everything from major to minor servicing was carried out by the unit. Behind the three main hangars was the engineering headquarters and storage hangars. The maintenance people fought a constant struggle to try and eek out remaining airframe hours from highly-fatigued aircraft, as individual Lightnings would often have hardly any of the latter left, but an abundance of the former! An aircraft in this situation could therefore be flown on a long sortie, but not pull any g. Conversely, a Lightning reaching the end of its airframe life might have hardly any flying hours left on it, but still have plenty of available g to pull! As well as looking after the engineering of the aircraft, the station also stocked all the RAF's reserves of Red

Top and Firestreak missiles. Located on the north east corner of the airfield, 'missile city' carried out all rectification work on the weapons.

The Lightning had been designed at the end of the 1950s when manpower was not a problem, and this was graphically shown by the fact that it could take several days to change an engine. With the unique arrangement of mounting the two engines on top of each other, there was little room left for fuel and hydraulic pipes. As a result, all these pipes were wrapped around potentially hazardous regions on the engines' outer casings, where the temperatures rose to extreme levels in flight. Both engine bays had fire detection and fire protection systems fitted, the latter comprising fire extinguishers which could be discharged into the affected area. Conversely, in the reheat zone there was fire detection but no fire protection! All you could do if a fire warning emanated from this segment of the engine bay was deselect reheat and hope for the best. In the early days a number of aircraft were lost through fuel leaks resulting in fires, and things got so bad that a standing joke at the time stated that if you wanted to purchase a Lightning, just buy some land near Spurn Point and one was bound to crash into it'. Legend also has it that the airways reporting point on the Lincolnshire coast which is now known as 'Silva' was initially called 'Silver Pit' because of the frequent Lightning crashes. This 'black period' peaked in 1971 when ten aircraft were lost, primarily through a lack of fire integrity checks. By the end of the decade all these problems had been ironed out, however, and although there was never room for complacency when flying the Lightning, the risk was greatly reduced because of the revised maintenance practices by then in place. Many modifications were made to the aircraft as a result of accident investigations. For example, the clean lines of the early F.1s were far removed from the later marks, which were covered in a multitude of vents

and drains that peppered the fuselage. As an example of the lengths engineers went to prevent fuselage fires, every time a fuel coupling was undone in the main fuel transfer system, it had to be x-rayed to ensure that it had been correctly refitted. Each squadron also had a specialist engineer who was tasked with checking all the systems after an engine or jet pipe was refitted.

Personally, as a junior pilot on the squadron, my favourite sight was walking through the hangar at the start of night flying to see the 'Tub' in the proverbial 'million pieces', as this signified that I was safe from having a no-notice night dual sortie with the squadron IWI or QFI sprung on me!

Often, if there was a shortage of single-seaters the most junior pilot would go off with a more experienced pilot in the right-hand seat. This was also the case if the weather was very bad, as having only around 300 hours of total flying time, all you

Binbrook's Lightning storage hangar. With the their former unit now disbanded, ex-No. 5 Sqn aircraft sit silently awaiting their final fates.

held was an instrument rating of battle green. This meant that on a live QRA mission you could fly down to a height of 200 ft on recovery to base, but on routine day-to-day sorties you had to work to the more restrictive white limit of a 400-ft cloud base. One way around this was to send you off in the T.5 with a right-hand seat qualified pilot, and then use his limit of 200 ft for recovery – every junior pilot's nightmare! This was why all the junior pilots liked to see the T.5 in pieces, safe in the knowledge that most fixes were not quick.

Without a shadow of a doubt, the Lightning must have been the most demanding aircraft in terms of maintenance ever operated by the RAF, and perhaps it was this challenge that endeared it to both air and ground crew alike. The Rolls-Royce Avons were very reliable and robust. Birdstrikes were never a problem in the Lightning – I can't recall ever seeing an airframe with any major damage after hitting a bird. Any birds that had gone down the intake were normally spat out the other end without affecting the turbine blades.

Each engine had a life of about 600 hours before it was changed and sent for servicing. The airframes themselves were given routine servicing every 75 hours, and a major service every 500 hours. A couple of aircraft had passed the 4,000-hour mark by the end of their lives, although most were around the 3,500-hour mark. The most frequently changed items on the aircraft were the high pressure tyres, which usually lasted a mere 10 to 15 sorties – this worked out at around a new tyre per week per wheel hub. The line crews who performed this routine after and before flight servicing were extremely slick at the task, turning a Lightning round ready for its next flight like grand prix mechanics in a pit lane. An example of their speed was shown during the last *Mallet Blow* exercise in which the LTF participated in 1987. During the preparation phase for the event it became clear that the Lightnings were going to engage their targets (Harrier GR.3s) some 100 miles out from Binbrook as they flew in from Germany. Unbeknown to the RAFG force, they would be engaged not once but *twice* by the same Lightnings. As soon as the first intercept had been effected, the fighters took their shots and turned for base at full speed.

Breaking quickly into the circuit and landing, the

XP693 flown by Colin Rae closes up on a Tornado F.3.

four Lightnings taxied back to the line to be met by the fastest turnaround crews on record. With the jet pipes still hot, 'chutes were refitted, fuel tankers connected up and engine oil levels checked. No sooner had the parking brakes been applied, than the familiar whee 'whoosh' of the Avpin starters brought the four-ship formation back to life. They were back airborne again in minutes, turning east and attacking the incoming bombers in the Binbrook overhead. They had been on the ground for less than ten minutes.

Structurally, the airframe was very much made in the mould of the Buccaneer – built to last. During its lifetime, the Lightning fleet was subjected to two major fatigue enhancement programmes to ensure that sufficient fatigue life remained until the end of

the airframes' life. In 1985 35 F.6s were put through the Mod 9 programme carried out by British Aerospace Warton. Most of these Lightnings survived until final retirement of the type in 1988, although three were lost in crashes. In short, this modification gave the aircraft an extra 400 hours flying time. The last major servicing undertaken at Binbrook was carried out in mid-1987, and took 30 weeks to complete. From that point on it was calculated that there was sufficient life left in the remaining airframes to last until retirement.

Aside from the fuel gauges, the other most utilized piece of equipment on the Lightning was the fatigue meter, this small black box showing all the counts of g pulled by the pilot on each sortie. On an average mission he might pull 2½g 15 times, 4g twice and

The last Lightning 'Diamond Nine' showing off to advantage the various colour schemes adopted across the fleet in its later years.

'Going Vertical'.

how much fatigue life they had left before they were to be withdrawn – all available fatigue was used up before the airframe was retired.

Plans had originally been drawn up for surplus Lightnings to be used as unmanned targets at Llanbedr, on the west Wales coast. Those aircraft earmarked for the programme had to keep half a unit of fatigue life left so that they could be flown to their new base from Binbrook, but in the end the project was cancelled – the thought of seeing a pilotless Lightnings trying to land on Llanbedr's crosswind-prone runway proved too hazardous.

Towards the end it was often acceptable to figuratively 'pull the wings' off on an aircraft that was about to be retired. It was quite easy to use one complete unit of fatigue during a 30-minute air combat sortie, and at that rate you could have used up an airframe in less than 100 hours! Some Lightning pilots had spent two or three years flying the aircraft in the late 1970s never pulling more than the bare minimum of g needed in an effort to make them last as long as they did, and I felt very humble arriving right at the end of the type's frontline life and being able to fly the aircraft to its design limits on virtually every sortie. In the last months of operations I flew over 30 air combat missions, which was more than some pilots had flown in several years of squadron flying.

True, the aircraft was difficult to maintain, but as more and more were retired, there slowly grew a ready supply of spares. In April 1988 one of the aircraft needed a generator change, and when a replacement arrived, its wooden packing case was date-stamped 1967 – parts had lain in store for 20 years at various depots throughout the country. Despite the challenge of working with valves when 'solid-state' was the in word, the Lightning's systems were reliable. There was a lot of truth in the saying that as long as you could get the aircraft started, nothing else would go wrong.

With the last Binbrook Open Day having come and gone, the squadrons carried on with their daily routines. Looking at facts and figures in my logbook for September 1987 provides a good guide as to the pace of life in this final Lightning autumn. In that

6g once, all this being recorded and added to the total from the previous flights. The overall life of the airframe was measured in units, 100 being the original maximum, but this was later increased after the modification programme. It was therefore possible to tell each pilot how much fatigue or airframe life he had used after each sortie, this in turn being displayed on a board in the ops room to inform each pilot just how much fatigue he had used each month. All aircraft also had a board showing month I flew 45 sorties, including a back-seat ride in an F-16 and the annual spinning exercise in the Jet Provost. Of the 43 Lightning missions, five were flown in the T.5 and the rest solo. At the end of September I'd amassed 210 hours on Lightnings over 12 months. I had flown three sorties in the same day on nine occasions that month, and on the 15th I went one better with four trips in the F.6. This was truly the end of an era, providing the best (and indeed the last) 'flying club' atmosphere within the frontline RAF.

No longer were sorties limited to intercepting straight and level non-evading targets. Now it was more a case of anything goes, with low-level overland combat air patrols against raids of Jaguars and Harriers being matched by similar sorties over the sea against other Lightnings that used every trick in the book to sneak up on you. As a new pilot on the squadron, my progress was being constantly monitored through the completion of periodic handling checks, initially flown every three months, but which were gradually extended to six months before finally becoming an annual check. In truth, these rides were generally a welcome break from the pressure of radar work, because part of the check ride consisted of low-level navigation, which came as a rare treat for air defence pilots.

The squadron QFI, Flt Lt Ian Hollingworth, also had a habit of making you fly ultra low-level circuits, which were entertaining. Normally, these were flown at 500 ft. However, rightly so the day you would do one for real the cloud base would be lower, so the QFI decided that it would be best to practice a couple at circuits at 250 ft.

I was always wary of QFIs, as I'd been caught out on the LTF by another of their ideas of fun. To further illustrate my point, I return briefly to my last weeks on the LTF. By mid-February 1987 I had finished all the radar work on the Lightning, and only had two or three air combat sorties left to complete prior to finishing the course. Typically, the weather over the Binbrook hill at this time of year was miserable, with thick fog offering no prospect of clearing in the foreseeable future. On the west coast it was wide open, so it was planned that two aircraft would deploy to RAF Valley and get the air combat syllabus finished. I'd be flying in the two-seater with a QFI, and one of the IWIs would take an F.3. The fog was so thick that from the crew room it was impossible to see the aircraft on the line 50 yards

Aircraft that had been lovingly cared for for over 25 years were quickly reduced to wrecks in a matter of minutes once the scrapmen were let loose inside Binbrook.

Bob Bees drinks a toast to celebrate his last Lightning sortie. Having spent many years at Binbrook, Bob clocked up over 1,000 hours on-type, and an ejection from XR760. He's still smiling because after finishing on the Lightning he had been posted to fly the F-15 Eagle at Tyndall Air Force Base in the US. To the right of the picture, Ian Hollingworth sports the latest in Lightning fashion – from October to May all over-sea sorties were flown wearing an immersion suit which, although cumbersome, was the most effective waterproof garment available.

away, and during the brief I became a little agitated when I saw that the flight leader had planned for a pairs close formation take-off – at best I might see his wing tip on the take-off roll. We walked to the aircraft, strapped in, started up and taxied out.

Keeping sight of the F.3 as it disappeared in and out of fog as we headed for the runway wasn't doing my nerves any good, and upon lining up ready for take-off, it was just possible to make out two sets of runway lights – the legal minimum. I could feel the tension building as my leader asked for clearance to take-off, and to my relief called for a 30-second stream departure. I was instantly filled with relief, and when we landed at Valley and met for the debrief, the instructors told me that they were testing me to see at what point I would 'chicken out'. Some test!

By the time October arrived, I had 38 more Lightning hours in my logbook, and I prepared to depart for Valley again, but this time with No. 11 Sqn. Each year all air defence units deploy to Strike Command's air-to-air missile establishment on the west Wales coast, where they are normally allocated about five live missiles to fire, thus giving frontline pilots a 50 per cent chance of participating in a live firing sortie. As this was to be the last Lightning Missile Practice Camp (MPC), the numbers of Red Top and Firestreak rounds made available to us was greatly increased. In fact, the real obstacle was the availability of targets, as each missile had to be fired at a flare towed behind a remote-controlled Jindivik target drone. The range encompasses most of Cardigan Bay, and is used not only by all three branches of the armed forces, but also by the

Ministry of Defence for procurement trials – indeed, range time for the testing of new weapons systems has priority over RAF needs. Therefore, despite the fact that No. 11 Sqn had an unlimited supply of missiles, trying to fire them all would be a difficult task.

Prior to deploying the Lightnings to Wales, a lot of behind the scenes work was carried out at Binbrook as the engineering team decided which aircraft to take. A record was kept of every Lightnings' individual missile firing history, and as far as it was possible, attempts were made to let each aircraft launch at least one missile during its life in order to check that the armament circuits functioned correctly. Certain aircraft were prone to radar failures, whilst others seemed to be jinxed mechanically, and despite the engineers best efforts, refused to fire.

Although the deployment was scheduled to last a fortnight, good weather usually ensured that the task would be finished earlier. However, it had been known for squadrons to land at Valley on the Monday and then depart two weeks later having not turned a wheel due to poor weather. Unlike modern missiles, the Red Top and Firestreak could only be fired outside cloud, and in winter, skies were rarely clear over the UK.

Normally, the squadron took five single-seaters and one two-seater to Wales, the presence of the latter aircraft allowing photo-chase work to be undertaken if required. On the aircrew front, a list of firing profiles available would be issued to the squadron IWI several months before the deployment. He would then compare this with his records detailing which pilots had fired what missiles, and accordingly draw up a crew list

XR725 looking resplendent at altitude.

Appearing to be well-satisfied with the results of a hectic one v one v one ACM sortie, a trio of pilots head back to the line hut.

showing those selected for the annual camp. Normal procedure was to give each pilot a primary profile to learn, as well as a secondary profile should conditions change. Each profile carried a code to enable you to determine the exact parameters of both the fighter and the target – for example, AB10 might indicate a fighter at 1,000 ft flying at 350 knots, and the target at 100 ft and 300 knots.

Once you were allocated your attack profile, you were packed off to the simulator to run through the whole set-up. The 'sim' allowed you to work through any potential pitfalls before performing the sortie in the air. Additionally, it gave you an accurate idea of how much fuel you would use should the

mission go according to plan. Having run through the attack a couple of times in the simulator, it was time to have a go at the same profile in the air. One aircraft would act as the Jindivik, whilst the other performed the role of the fighter. You would then swap around, possibly changing profiles. Back on the ground, Friday afternoons were reserved for lectures given by either the squadron IWI or operational pilots on the various weapons systems. Detailed briefings were performed on both types of missile and the radar itself, and following two weeks of detailed lectures, you felt like you could literally take the missile apart and rebuild it yourself.

Once all the aircraft had flown to Valley, it was

quickly decided which pilots were to fire in the first range slot. A typical Lightning firing would involve up to three pilots to fire one missile. The lead pilot briefed the departure from Valley and the transit to the holding gate – a small island off the Lleyn Peninsular. The second Lightning, and its pilot, acted as an airborne spare, whilst the third pilot would act as a ground spare. Up to a certain point, he could replace either aircraft in case of unserviceability. Having got to the holding gate, the spare Lightning was forced to either orbit at height or stay with the primary aircraft until the missile left the rail. As the cockpit was so cramped, all that you could carry on a live firing exercise was a small green 'Noddy' guide booklet, which contained all the details of the firing parameters. Upon leaving the holding gate at your assigned time, you changed radio frequencies so as to establish contact with the range controller. Now adopting your single letter callsign, the stress level increased exponentially, as any error you now

made would be seen by dozens of people, and your name would be in lights at Group Headquarters at Bentley Priory – the onus was squarely on you to get it right.

Everything in the range was done with reference to timing, so as soon as your controller told you 'Alpha minus five', you would hit your stopwatch. At each stage in the lead up to missile launch you verified with your check list that you had carried out all the necessary pre-firing procedures – had you selected the right weapon, was it armed and was the radar in the right mode? On my firing mission all was going smoothly until the last couple of minutes. My profile was to be flown at 500 ft, at which height I would fire a Red Top against a target flying at 300 knots and 100 ft. My speed would be 350 knots, so I'd have around 50 knots of overtake on the Jindivik.

It was the controller's job to make sure that we were set up line astern at five miles on the correct

Photographed in typical Welsh weather, the crews that participated in the last Lightning MPC look suitably solemn. From left to right, the Author, Paul Cooper, Dick Coleman, Richard Learner, (Squadron Engineering Officer), Bob Bees and Steve Hunt. In civilian clothes the British Aerospace representative Dave Hart, and Simon Braithwaite. The inscription reads 'The Last Lightning MPC 1963-1987'. 'God have pity on those who follow'.

Night close formation take-offs were forbidden, and this launch must have been just on the time limit. Two No. 11 Sqn Lightnings roll down the RAF Valley runway on their way back to Binbrook.

attack heading running in on the target – on his radar scope he would be watching the Jindivik and my Lightning to ensure that we were aligned on the right course. The former was being flown remotely by a controller on the ground at Llanbedr.

As we got down to minus two minutes, the controller was still giving me small heading changes. It was important to fly the aeroplane as accurately as possible. Looking desperately in the radar for the target, I still could not see anything. It was now just two miles ahead of me. At one-and-a-half miles, 30 seconds before trigger press, I still could not see him, so I locked up and looked out. Time was now rapidly running out when I heard 'alpha flares lit',

so I made the trigger live and scanned the skies in desperation, looking for the burning flares – try as I might, I still couldn't see them.

I expected the target to be on my nose, so it came as something of a surprise when I caught sight of the flares well to my port side. I immediately called back 'Alpha visual'. Knowing I had only had a few seconds in which to fire, I turned hard after the flares to bring them back onto my nose. On my starboard wing was a Hawk filming the shot for a video to be released later that year, and its pilot desperately tried to stay with me as I banked hard left then corrected right. The flare was now right in my gunsight, and with the missile acquired, I squeezed the trigger. After what seemed an age, but was in reality probably less than a second, the missile accelerated off the port rail. The cockpit was filled with a tremendous whooshing noise as I watched the weapon speed straight for the flare. I rolled right to keep clear of the debris hemisphere, and thus allowing the Hawk to film the impact. Dropping a wing, I saw a puff of black smoke as the missile exploded – a direct hit had been registered. I gave the code word that my missile had left the rail and that all my switches were safe.

The flare burn time on the Jindivik was around 20 seconds, and I had fired at 15 – another couple of seconds and the controller would have called 'Wait, Wait, Wait', which was the signal not to fire. The primary reason why the controller kept a close watch on the flare's burn time was that should a

pilot fire just as the flare went out, there was every chance that the missile's seeker head would transfer to the Jindivik, and thus destroy the drone.

Keeping visual with the Hawk, I turned towards the Jindivik to check that it was undamaged, for despite the fact that the flare burned on a tow wire some distance behind the drone, there was always the chance that it could have been damaged. To attempt to recover a damaged target was deemed to be too dangerous, as a crash on approach or landing was considered to be the most likely outcome of such a venture. If this was the case, the Jindivik would have to be abandoned over the sea. After checking that 'my' drone was undamaged, I still had enough fuel left to make a quick approach to Llanbedr before the Jindivik was recovered.

As I arrived in the vicinity of the airfield, I was

'Store Away'. Dick Heath squeezes the trigger to initiate one of the last Red Top firings.

Pulling hard in combat, the wings of XR753 produce a shroud of mist as the lift breaks away.

'burners in, stood the Lightning on its tail, and ran for home like a scalded cat – I should have known better. Due to a variety of factors the last Lightning MPC took the full two weeks, and we stayed until 16 October 1987.

In an effort to use up the remaining fatigue life of the aircraft, more and more air combat training sorties were being flown as the end drew near. The Lightning possessed some fairly unique qualities in combat, as it was a big, powerful and thirsty aeroplane that could optimize the tremendous excess thrust it possessed. On the negative side, it had a weapons system that was virtually prehistoric, a high wing loading and a cockpit that was surrounded by ironmongery.

Two types of scenario could be played out when indulging in air combat – 'Heaters and Guns' or 'Guns only', the latter being the 'sport of kings' for fighter pilots. In the first scenario, you had to position the Lightning in a rear hemisphere envelope, working out to about two miles and around 40° off the tail to achieve a kill – just like a high level or supersonic intercept. The missile envelopes varied with target altitude, speed and g. To claim a 'Guns' kill you needed either a steady tracking shot of two seconds at 300 yards, or two snapshots – the latter saw you 'hose' the bullets across the target's flightpath in the hope that one or two would hit. Steady tracking saw you put the pipper on the target's back and 'track like a God'. Most tracking shots were a 'feeling the water' type attack with the Lightning, and involved only 10 per cent aiming. You had to be able to put your bullets ahead of the 'bandit', leading his move. In the immortal words of one American pilot, 'There is no kill like a "Guns" kill'.

Prior to the commencement of each air combat mission, a lengthy briefing was carried out, during which it became evident that we were moving up a gear in terms of aircraft employment. No longer would it be target v fighter at pre-briefed heights and speeds like in the early days of the Lightning. Now it was a pair of pilots rushing towards each other, each with a fighting spirit that dictated that you must not lose at almost any cost. The aircraft

treated to a rare sight. Still in use at this far-flung outpost were a couple of long-forgotten fighter types in the shape of the Meteor and Sea Vixen, their job being to 'shepherd' the pilotless drones and help the ground controllers recover them. At about two miles distance, dead ahead, I identified a red and yellow Sea Vixen, its twin boom tail being instantly recognizable. I wondered if its pilot was up for a spot of fun, and turning in behind him, I tried to get some gun film of this equally ancient fighter from my veteran mount. He spotted me straight away, however, and aware of my game, he suddenly turned hard into me. I was completely taken aback as the aircraft's turn rate was excellent, and very soon we passed each other head on. Discretion being the better part of valour, I immediately knew I'd bitten off more that I could chew and 'plugged' both was going to have every ounce of energy wrung out of it, the g meter would be at its limit and the speed was liable to go off the scale. To get your prized kill you had to get in there and 'mix it up' with your adversary, as no one ever scored a kill doing a rate one turn!

Even on a simple Lightning v Lightning sortie, it was still a requirement that all the rules of the flight be thoroughly briefed prior to take-off. The engagement had to take place in clear airspace away from built-up areas – preferably over the sea. The base height for operational pilots was 5,000 ft, which was close enough to the ground to keep the mind concentrated when embroiled in a dogfight. A vital point was the minimum separation brief – 1,000 ft, or the '1,000-ft bubble', as it was known. Passing another Lightning just 1,000 ft away when you are both doing 650 mph is enough to make any pilot's eyes water. A mandatory part of each briefing

was the spin recovery drill, as if you were ever going to spin in a Lightning, this was the most likely time for it to occur. Nose high, no airspeed, lots of roll input and a fair amount of rudder – every Lightning pilot has been there.

Unlike modern fly-by-wire 'electric' fighters, there was no angle-of-attack limit in the Lightning, so all aggressive manoeuvring was pure 'seat of the pants' stuff, with a sixth sense telling you when to back off. If you did get into a spin and the aircraft hadn't recovered by 10,000 ft, then the only way out was to eject. If you did mishandle the aircraft and spin, then the rule was to return to base once you had recovered. The chances were the aircraft may have suffered some structural damage either in the air combat leading up to its departure from controlled flight, or in the spin itself – indeed, the former may have been the cause of the spin in the first place.

Fuel awareness also now became crucial, as the

'A £25 million Tornado F.3 is gunned by a 2/6d Lightning' – that was what some wag wrote alongside this picture when it was left in the No. 11 Sqn crewroom.

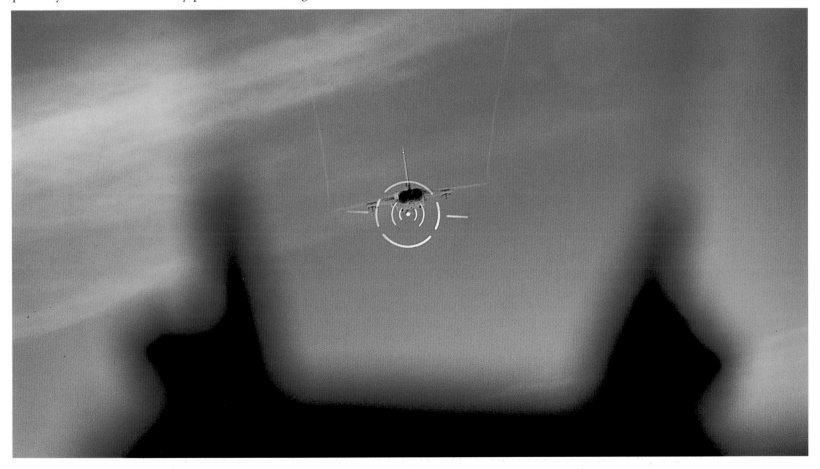

Lightning wasn't equipped with fancy audio warnings that told you when critical fuel states had been reached. On a normal mission three calls were made – 'Ventral', 'Bingo 1' and 'Bingo 2'. The first call indicated that your ventral tank was empty and that you could now work to the higher g limit, whilst the 'Bingo' calls signified pre-arranged fuel states which allowed the leader to be aware of his wingman's remaining fuel. 'Bingo 2' could also dictate a reheat cut, meaning that sufficient fuel remained for dry power only.

Initially, during the work-up phase all junior pilots performed a one v one combat sortie with the squadron weapons officer, or a senior pilot. These were relatively short sorties of around 20 minutes' duration. Once you were cleared solo, an F.6 ACT (Air Combat Training) mission was flown which lasted 25 to 30 minutes, the trip being arranged, if possible, in conjunction with a standard tanking sortie. The most ambitious missions of all, however, were those that involved a maximum of four v four, although these were somewhat rare.

In combat, pilots would either fly an 'energy fight' or an 'angles fight'. In the first case it was a matter of keeping your speed up around 360 knots at all times, as this was the Lightning's best cornering speed – any faster and you could use some of this potential energy in the vertical plane, always controlling the buffet carefully. An important factor in successfully combating the Lightning focused on controlling the level of buffet, which again was all down to feel. If you pulled too hard the aircraft went into deep buffet, thus degrading your energy levels very quickly, but if this resulted in you achieving a firing position, then all well and good. However, if it did not, all you ended up doing was bleeding off your speed and energy, and thus putting yourself behind the drag curve at the mercy of your opponent. Knowing when to pull hard and when to keep your energy is a skill known only to fighter pilots.

The 'angles fight' was performed by the more gifted Lightning pilots, trying to capitalize on their opponent's errors and being patient. Something that would always take an opponent by surprise was the

aeroplane's ability to stand on its tail at very low speed. Looping in the Lightning was banned for a very long time due to fears that structural loads placed on the fin during this manoeuvre would prove to be too great for the vertical surface to withstand. Ironically, the loop later proved to be one of the most widely-used tactics in air combat, as it allowed you to rapidly gain the upper hand by climbing above your opponent, and then allowing your nose to slice down onto him. Great care was needed not to 'bury' the nose, for if you allowed it to go too far below the horizon it was very hard to get it back up again, despite the huge amounts of thrust available from the two Avons engines. This was due largely to the Lightning's relatively small tailplane, the effectiveness of which could also be masked by the wing. In dissimilar air combat, the Lightning could hold its own against the Phantom II and Harrier GR.3, but was outclassed by the F-15 and F-16.

Some of the most demanding combat sorties I was ever involved in were performed as part of a three-ship formation. Each pilot flew to the centre-point of a circle, which had a radius of ten miles. Passing over the centre, the leader called 'outwards turn', upon which each pilot flew off in a direction 120°

One of the few occasions when Tornados and Lightnings flew together in formation was in March 1988.

LAST OF THE LIGHTNINGS

For the last of the Lightning pilots, refuelling from a Buccaneer was an uncommon event. Seen here is the company-owned XP693, flown by Peter Gordon Johnson, taking on fuel from a Buccaneer flown by Keith Hartley. Awaiting his turn is fellow Binbrook pilot Alan Page in XR773 'BR'.

away from the next Lightning. On reaching the edge of the circle, all 'players' turned inbound again to cross the centre-point, and thus the fight became 'live'. Each pilot then went about employing every sneaky trick he knew to claim the first kill, the aim of the sortie being to teach each pilot how to try and survive in a high-threat environment. With the introduction of GCI, it became an excellent way of improving a pilot's 'situational awareness'. As soon as you became 'live', and found another Lightning either visually or on radar, it took great discipline to take just a quick shot at your foe and then clear the area. All the time your head was turning, scanning for the third aircraft. In terms of providing pilot satisfaction, the Lightning was hard to equal when flown in the air combat environment.

With the arrival of the new year, the Binbrook Lightning force had just four months of operational flying left. This was a busy period for No. 11 Sqn, who maintained a hectic operational schedule right to the end. In January four F.6s and a T.5 were sent to Gutersloh for Dissimilar Air Combat Training with the Harrier GR.3s, thus marking the last occasion that frontline Lightnings operated over Germany. As well as flying against the Harriers in combat, the opportunity was also taken to fly some low-level missions when the weather permitted. At the time heavy snow had fallen on the North German plain, and some of No. 4 Sqn's Harriers were decorated in a washable white and grey camouflage scheme – it was only due to the intervention of our squadron warrant officer that one of our Lightnings escaped being repainted in a similar scheme. The detachment proved a great success, with several sorties flown along the Osnabruck ridge – a familiar hunting ground for the F.2s from a bygone era.

Returning to the UK, preparations were already well advanced with the overwing tanks programme. With severe delays occurring with the introduction of the Tornado F.3's radar, more and more trials were being flown in an effort to rectify the

Holding a knife edge position, the pilot of XS928 shows off the large over-wing tanks to advantage.

problems, and a decision had been made to refurbish six F.6s and fit them once again with the overwing fuel tanks. Dubbed 'over burgers', once these tanks were fitted they couldn't be jettisoned as the explosive release mechanisms originally fitted to the stores had been rendered inoperable. Normally two aircraft were deployed to Warton for a week at a time, where they operated alongside the resident XP693 and the company-owned Buccaneer. All the missions were flown over the Aberporth range against one of the development Tornados, or a

highly-modified Buccaneer fitted with Foxhunter radar. Rigged for refuelling, the British Aerospace Buccaneer tanker also gave pilots the chance to do some air-to-air refuelling over the range – with the refuelling pod on the right wing and the Lightning's probe on the left, it meant that your cockpit got very close to the Buccaneer's tail when 'plugged in'.

Sometimes, the missions were relatively complex, with up to four targets flying low over the sea in typically inclement Welsh weather. Each run would see you execute pre-briefed evasion at certain

152

distances in order to ascertain whether the Foxhunter could track evading targets. By the end of March most of the trials flying was being performed by crews from Warton, who now operated a total of four F.6s.

The last Lightning delivered back to the factory was XS928, flown in by Flt Lt 'Porky' Page on 13 June 1988. Initially, the refurbished Lightnings were to stay in service for a maximum period of two years, but this was eventually extended to nearly five – the last flight finally took place in January 1993. One aircraft was stored for over a year at Boscombe Down, but was eventually put back into service when XR724's fatigue life ran out.

At the end of their lives all four aircraft were preserved, XP693 and XR773 being delivered to Exeter in December 1992 – they have since been maintained in airworthy condition in the hope that one day clearance will be given to allow them to fly. Of the others, XR724 went back to Binbrook to also be retained in airworthy condition (it therefore holds the distinction of being the last Lightning to land at the base), XS928 was kept at Warton for display and XS904 – the last ever Lightning to fly – was delivered to Bruntingthorpe. Once again it is kept in working order, and is regularly taxied with along with its sister-ship XR728.

April 1988 saw the Lightning finally bow out of operational service, No. 11 Sqn being non-declared to NATO as of the last day of that month. Preparations had been in hand for several months organizing the events to mark the end of the Lightning, and despite the dwindling numbers of remaining aircraft, it was decided to put up one last 'Diamond Nine'. Sufficient single-seaters were available to make up the formation, plus provide the

Looking more like the Neanderthal man picking at the bones of a prehistoric animal, a scrapman helps 'devour' a Lightning T.5. Having acted as a decoy for ten years, this aircraft unceremoniously had its tail removed before being rolled onto its back to await the cutter's torch. Fuel can be seen streaming from split tanks across its spine and fuselage.

odd spare. Doubt then still existed as to the fate of the aircraft after the 1 May retirement date, and at one point it looked as though a few of the two-seaters would end up in the USA as high-speed chase aircraft, but in the end this came to nothing.

The distinction of leading the final 'Diamond Nine' went to Wg Cdr Jake Jarron, the No. 11 Sqn boss. Leading and briefing a large group of fighters demands meticulous preparation. Safety aspects are thoroughly discussed, and decisions made as to who will do what in the event of an emergency. Equally important was the looser plan, which detailed what would happen should one or more aircraft go unserviceable either in the air or on the ground. Particular emphasis was placed on the position of the photo-chase aircraft, ensuring that he was always a safe distance from the formation.

Following one practice sortie on the 28th, the main flypast took place the following day. The whole event went without a hitch, and so ended the Lightning legend. The squadron now had two months to wrap everything up, deliver aeroplanes around the world and close the station. The final deployment took place in May when two F.6s and two T.5s deployed to RAF Lossiemouth, in the north of Scotland, for one last joint affiliation exercise.

Working with No. 12 Sqn's Buccaneers and Hunters once again, the Lightnings performed combat air patrols over the North Cape. With unlimited visibility and no airspace restrictions, the conditions were ideal for the ageing fighter. With large formations of Buccaneers coming in from the west, the Lightnings put up high-level CAPs on the north-west coast in the hope of catching the low-level package with an unseen attack. Sitting just below the contrails at around 30,000 ft, you could see right across Scotland as for once there was no cloud. Looking down over land at this height, there was no way the radar would detect the incoming bombers, so the only option was to try and pick up the shadows flashing over the ground which, hopefully, would ultimately lead our eyes onto the prey. Acquiring an early visual contact on our adversaries, we selected the throttles to idle and

With its squadron markings removed, XS928 nevertheless still manages to look pristine on its last RAF flight. Just forward of the wing is a small orange sticker which reads 'property of the Royal Danish Air Force' – a reminder of an earlier squadron exchange.

Leading a 'Diamond Nine' of Lightnings was not an everyday event, and the briefing had to be thorough and meticulous in order to cover every eventuality. Jake Jarron stands proudly in front of his work of art, having briefed the nine pilots who took part in the flypast.

With only 24 hours left of Lightning operations, No. 11 Sqn's hangar looks rather empty. By the following evening both these F.6s would also be gone for ever.

rolled inverted, diving on our prey. With our radars silent, the Buccaneers had no indications on their radar warning receivers to our imminent attack. We slipped in behind the back pair and claimed our shots – we had been totally undetected. The element of surprise arriving from high after a visual committal had caught them off guard.

The next mission saw the Buccaneers in their element low over the sea attacking ships. Our task was to man a four-ship CAP and try and pick them up, either on radar or visually. The attackers were flying at 100 ft, and our 'hard deck' minimum was 250 ft, so we weren't going to be able to 'skyline' them. The cloud base was lowering over the Moray Firth as we set up our pattern, and our leader – an experienced pilot – soon found them on radar. Shortly after this his wingman almost became another statistic of the dangerous profession of fast jet flying. Skimming across the waves at low-level trailing the lead Lightning, he heard the contact call and looked into his scope, but to no avail. Suddenly, he felt the sea rushing towards him – just a feeling – and instinctively he pulled, taking his head out of the scope. He told me much later that all he could see was water all around him, looking very close and very black – he dare not say how low he was. Over-confidence with the aircraft had almost cost him his life, as he had spent just a second too long with his head in the scope. By the time we found the targets it was too late as they had got past us. Very quickly the detachment was over, and it was time to head south.

In the month of May three of the squadron's aircraft were delivered to bases in RAF Germany to be used as decoys. The longest delivery flight

performed by any of our F.6s was that undertaken by XS929, which went back to Cyprus to act as a gate guardian for RAF Akrotiri. Accompanied by two T.5s and two VC10 tankers, the aircraft was placed on permanent display at the base – this particular Lightning was an appropriate choice, as it had once served on the island with No. 56 Sqn.

By the end of June 1988 there were only a handful of Lightnings left in service. Most of the pilots had moved onto other types, and the station was running down. In a low key ceremony, the last two Lightnings left the base at the end of June, flown by two long-time Lightning pilots, Sqn Ldrs

Paul Cooper and John Aldington. With all the ground equipment cleared away for the last time, they came back low across the dispersal for a final flypast, before climbing away to be delivered to their new owner. Sadly, plans to put both aircraft on the civil register failed to materialize, and they were scrapped along with a number of other ex-Binbrook Lightnings at Cranfield in December 1994.

The final phasing out of the Lightning was now complete, and a significant chapter in the RAF's history came a close. Sadly, I've never seen, or flown, anything quite like the Lightning since the summer of 1988, and I don't suppose I ever will . . .

Gone but not forgotten, the legend lives on.

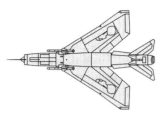

CHAPTER 5

Lightning Flashback

'**D**o you fancy a flight in the Lightning this afternoon?'

I paused, but not for long. 'Yeah, brilliant, love to!'

'I'm going to do an aeros practice in about an hour if you want to come.'

I had known Mike Beachy Head, the owner of Thunder City, for a couple of years and had steadily grown to respect this larger than life character. A genuine South African, I'd met him in a windswept hangar at Plymouth some years before when I was on my way back from a dunking in the Atlantic Ocean as part of my Tornado reserve pilot training. I had called past to see Barry Pover, who was then the owner of Lightning T5, XS451, which

Halcyon days and time to reflect. The last days of Lightning operations at Binbrook. In the single-seat Lightning, the bond between man and machine was never closer.

was undergoing a rebuild to flying condition at Plymouth. Mike was quick to tell me he'd just bought this aircraft from Barry along with two single-seaters and another T5. I listened as his plans unfolded, all impressive stuff I thought, but like others I suspected that it would be a long haul. I offered him my help in any way, but I had to admit that I thought his chances were slim. As I got to know him it quickly became apparent that if any one individual could succeed where others have failed, it was Mike. His vision and drive are lessons to us all – the phrase 'failure is not an option' sums him up.

I'd flown my last Lightning sortie in an F6, XR754, in June 1988. It was a classic mission: three

Lightnings versus four Tornado F3s and four F-15 Eagles. It had been a great mission that culminated in a guns kill on an F-15 Eagle – the Lightning excelled to the end. The sortie over, I'd signed the Form 700 and taken the long walk back to the line hut like David Beckham when he was sent off in the match against Argentina. My dream was over. The open affair I had savoured with this racy lady was at an end and through no fault of my own. I had openly flaunted our relationship but now all that was left were the memories.

The years passed. I flew the vapid Tornado ADV and the exhilarating Mirage 2000 – a Lightning in French disguise that was sheer excitement. I'd flown

Pilots are indeed privileged people. Once in a while you witness sights that mere earthbound mortals will never see, but can only imagine. Coming off the tanker prior to a 2-v-2 combat sortie, the leader called the formation into line astern for the benefit of my camera. The rarely seen lenticular clouds add to the magic of this image.

Learning to fly. Sitting next to a seasoned Lightning pilot for 40 minutes on a radar sortie in a T5 was a sobering experience. Getting to grips with this beast of an aircraft was another matter. It's easy to see from this view how the aircraft gained the nickname of 'Tub'.

200 live combat missions over the Gulf during 'Desert Shield', 'Deny Flight' in Bosnia and again in 'Southern Watch' over Iraq. But nothing ever came close to an hour in a Lightning. I'd seen Russian 'Bears' in the Iceland gap, gunned F-16s, flown back-seat in Hornets, Eagles and Falcons. I'd flown fighters across the globe, done Red Flag, the Falklands and the Tactical Fighter Meet. But still my mind wandered back to the smell of Avpin, the leather seat cushion, and the raw power of the twin Avons. In all honesty it was impossible to substitute the thrill of flying an aircraft cherished by

generations of fighter pilots. What more could any self-respecting man dream of than strapping a Lightning to his back and flying a one-versus-one combat sortie above an English airfield at the height of summer?

Fifteen years later I donned that familiar flying kit – suit, gloves, G-suit and Mae West. This time, appropriately, I kept my cowboy boots on. Mike gave me a brief on what he planned to do and we walked out to the Tub. I'd seen Mike display his Hunter F6 with precision and poise so I was in no doubt of his flying ability. At that time, Thunder

LAST OF THE LIGHTNINGS

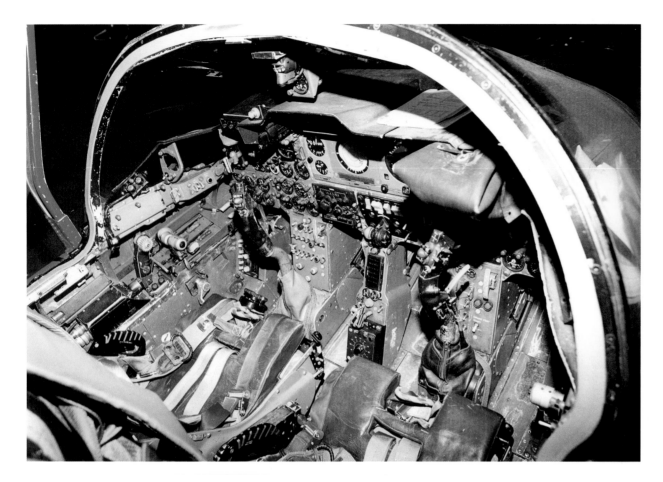

A cockpit view of T5, XS452, as she is today. Little has changed over the past 40 years. The rubber radar boot is missing from the left-hand side, although this considerably improves forward visibility. In its place are new radios and transponder equipment.

City had just one T5 airworthy which was the all-black XS452. I'd flown this aircraft on fifty previous occasions so she was no stranger. In fact I'd taken both my father and brother flying in this very aircraft that made her almost family (my mother had flown in a different T5, but that's another story!). She looked good in gloss black and had lost none of her military poise. Even devoid of weapons she still looked aggressive. I climbed the ladder as Mike performed the walk around. With a flood of nostalgia washing over me I climbed into the familiar cockpit and checked the Martin Baker ejector seat. It looked pristine, obviously given the care and respect it deserved. Squeezing into the right-hand seat the ergonomics, or rather the lack of them, hit me like a 50-ton truck. A mass of dials and instruments, some round and some rectangular, were scattered around the cockpit. The scene looked like

something from a Jules Verne novel. I strapped myself in, taking care to get the straps in the correct order. Leg restraints followed. Mike arrived and followed suit.

'OK, she's all yours,' he entreated.

The mental cogs turned slowly as I performed the left to right checks in the time-honoured fashion. I followed the principle of 'if its shiny and worn it needs to be up and on'. The cockpit of XS452 had changed little. The radar was gone from the left-hand side, replaced instead by modern radios, but otherwise it was still much the same. With the checks complete, Mike waved a single finger in the air to indicate to the ground crew that we were ready to start the number one engine.

People stood back as I pulled up the gang bar and pushed the start switch. The Lightning start-up sequence has been well documented, but suffice it to

XS452 was no stranger to me: I'd flown her fifty times before and taken both my father and brother up in her, too.

say that behind me a small quantity of highly combustible mono-fuel had been squirted into the starter unit, compressed, then ignited, and the resultant contained explosion brought the number one Avon growling to life. Ground power was waved away and we went through the same procedure to start the number two engine. Like everything else to do with the Lightning, the starting system is eccentric. The fuel source, Avpin, is now only manufactured in India and is phenomenally expensive – in fact it's so dear that it would probably be cheaper to use Chateau Haut Mabuzet instead! With both engines turning we waved away the chocks and closed the lid. Only then did I fully appreciate the awesome responsibility of flying a Lightning. Surrounded by steel and feeling very claustrophobic the whole experience is both intimidating and electric. You can feel the Lightning straining at the leash, rushing you to get airborne.

The fuel gauge was on the move now and any time wasted was precious fuel burnt. Mike called for taxi clearance and I released the brakes. I have to confess that I'd forgotten how hard the Lightning was to taxi; another ten trips and I reckon I'd have cracked it! Designed in an era when comfort and visibility were not essential items for a fast jet pilot, the view from the front was like looking through the slit in a pillar box. We taxied past rows of Boeing 737s and 747s against whose gargantuan bulk we seemed tiny. As we sat at the holding point I was amazed that I could actually watch the fuel gauge registering a drop. Who could have designed such a machine? But now we are ready to go.

We line up on Cape Town's wide runway and Mike brings up the power. All looks good as he hands me control. Acceleration is brisk and obvious. I lift the nose and wait for 170kts and then apply a good wedge of back stick. The Tub seems reluctant

162

LAST OF THE LIGHTNINGS

Rolling over the top. An unusual plan view of the T5.

A wide-angle lens makes the normally sleek Lightning look stubby.

to part company with terra firma and seems to raise her nose slightly in response. Mike swiftly brings the gear up and I hold her down. Not wishing to embarrass myself by pulling the stick hard back, I opt for a punchy turn away from the field, pulling the stick back briskly while simultaneously applying a good deal of right bank. This is no Mirage 2000 and even at 300kts with a straight hard wing and no lift augmentation devices we go straight into buffet, quite normal for a seasoned Lightning driver. I'm not used to the sensation and immediately ease off the back- pressure. Instantly the buffet stops and we skid round the corner. This fighter needs to be flown....

I push my right hand forward and the surge of power is impressive as we pass through 400kts. It's time to throttle back. The ventral tank is now empty and all we have is the wing fuel and a small amount in the flaps. Two giant hands in the shape of Avon 302s are pushing us along.

Beneath us the scenery is breathtaking: Table Mountain below, with the Atlantic Ocean away to our right and the Indian Ocean to our left. Beyond the end of the world, it doesn't get any better than this. We are level at 1,500ft and 450kts.

My fellow airline pilots far below, mere earthbound mortals on a 'stopover' lounging beside their hotel pools, look skywards and wish, 'if only…'.

As we coast out, Mike taps the burners and we surge forward. Roaring like a white lion we are soon hitting 600kts at 250ft. Maximum adrenaline kicks in as the burners are taken out and we reach for the big blue. Rotating the Tub around its axis we're soon at 10,000ft and heading back to the coast. We still have a healthy speed on the ASI, but if we'd done the same trick in the mighty Tornado we'd be unloading, plugging the burners back in and trying to regain lost energy.

Mike lets me fly her again and I run through my repertoire of manoeuvres. I'm not a QFI (Qualified Flying Instructor) or test pilot so therefore I avoid canned aerobatics and taking notes. Instead I pull to the buffet, turning hard, flowing from wing over to the next. I try to get the feel of this lady through my hands: stable, responsive and docile. The delights of combating such an awesome beast come flooding back. As a teaching aid she's second to none and with no head-up display it's just raw seat-of-the-pants flying. I try a level turn on instruments: it's hard work but achievable and far more satisfying than flying a head-up display. I think of the new generation of test pilots, all steely-eyed killers, masters of the electronic age, how they must be brought down to earth with a jolt when they're flying this fifties fighter.

Back to the present, or past, I hand control back to Mike and he runs through his aeros sequence. It's smooth and graceful and blissfully safe. I never have a doubt that I'm not in capable hands. We are down to 1,600lbs of fuel and it's time to go home. Mike

Tooling along with the Indian ocean below us, it doesn't get any better than this. Thunder City's F6, XR773, in 11 Squadron markings as 'BR'.

hands control back to me and I point the nose towards Cape Town's long runway. If nothing else, Lightning pilots always know which way to point. I can see the airfield ahead at about 25 miles range. We have to hold off as a South African Airways Jumbo comes into land. I come back to 300kts and set up a hold, ever conscious of the fuel dwindling away. As we line up on the runway Mike asks me if I want to land. I'm flattered but decline. Sitting in the right-hand seat my ambidextrous skills are not what they were and after all it's his baby.

As we come back to threshold speed at 500ft I'm amazed at the forward view, the speed doesn't seem high but then again the runway is almost as wide as most RAF runways are long! As we cross the threshold Mike brings the power back and we kiss the tarmac – it's a testament to his ability that we don't arrive 'air force' style burning the Dunlops. That final tweak of back stick seems to cushion the blow. As we vacate the runway I take control again, bringing the power up. Mike's eagle eye spots the rising JPT (it rises faster than the RPM). I'd forgotten old engines need respect. We taxi back after just 35 minutes airborne.

As I put the pins back in the seat I paused to think of the last 35 minutes, trying to savour the moment. The joy of flying a Lightning again – I'm thrilled by the whole experience, just as I was the first time some fifteen years before. Thunder City have proved that the impossible is possible. They have become the centre of excellence for jet warbird operations and justifiably so. Mike and his team have done an outstanding job. It was twelve years since I'd last flown the Lightning, but in the meantime I'd flown over 2,000hrs on the Tornado and Mirage 2000. Many of those hours were but a distant memory when compared to those 35 minutes in a Lightning that are now etched into my memory for many years to come.

There was never such a charismatic fighter as the Lightning, and there never will be again. I'm indebted to Thunder City for allowing me to relive the moment. Thank you, Mike.

CHAPTER 6

Lightnings on Civvie Street

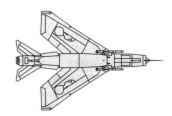

Mike Beachy Head's Story

It was in January 1995 that I first clapped eyes on the English Electric Lightning in the flesh, and what an imposing sight it was. There are few things on planet earth that intimidate me, but I have to admit that this awesome beast did just that, sitting menacingly in Barry Povers' Classic Jets Company hangar at Exeter in South Devon. Having just bought two Hawker Hunters and an English Electric Canberra at a Sotheby's auction in November 1994, I had arrived in England to view the aircraft and commence training on Hunters, as well as to prepare the aircraft for their transit flight back to my home at Cape Town in South Africa.

I suppose I had been the archetypal little boy,

Thunder City's F6, XP693, never entered squadron service but was retained as a trials aircraft at BAe Warton. Seen here at Warton as a Tornado takes off, Peter Gordon Johnson and I wait for our turn to act as targets.

having built aircraft models and hung them from my ceiling from an early age. The Lightning was always amongst them and now to see the real aircraft close up, albeit in static condition, was quite a moment. Barry invited me to climb up the ladder and sit in the cockpit of F6, XP693, the all silver ex-BAe aircraft. I spent a long time soaking up the aura of the beast, trying to imagine what it must be like sitting astride 35,000lb of thrust inside this tiny cockpit, hurtling through the ether at a great height. Climbing out of the cockpit and down the seemingly endless ladder, I stood and stared at her for another eternity. It was then that I said to Barry, 'I want one.'

At that moment I had no idea of what those three fateful words would come to mean. They set off a chain of events that were to cause great sorrow, joy, challenge, achievement and hardship, something that few could ever imagine.

Based at Exeter and in a complete but un-

airworthy state, were XP693 and XR773, both of them F6 single-seaters. Also part of Barry's outfit but stored at Plymouth Executive Aviation was T5, XS451, although she was in a state of considerable disrepair. Clearly, if I was going to get anywhere with the project a good two-seater was essential. But none of Barry's Lightnings were flyable at this stage.

The only other T5 we knew of was an ex-Arnold Glass aircraft based at Cranfield. It was being operated by Tony Hulls and a group of enthusiasts for fast taxi runs on weekends. We got hold of Tony who agreed to enter into discussions and I flew over to Cranfield in late 1995 to see him and the aircraft. In the meantime, contact had been made with the South African CAA (SA CAA) to ascertain whether we could operate the aircraft on the civil register.

Robbie Robinson, who was then the SA CAA Chief Flying Inspector, accompanied me on the trip to see Tony and T5, XS452. Tony and his team had been doing a sterling job of keeping the aircraft

The short-lived tail markings, BS (with all their connotations), were soon removed for obvious reasons.

Classic Binbrook. A pair of single-seaters taxi back, their mission accomplished.

running, albeit on bunker fuel, but nonetheless it was a sad sight to see this beautiful aircraft standing outside in the harsh British winter, covered only by a few tarpaulins and some tyres to weight them down. The tarps were removed, the aircraft fuelled up and prepared for a taxi run and Keith Hartley, the BAe test pilot, arrived to do the honours. This was essentially for my benefit, but would you buy a used car without a little test drive?

The cockpit was even smaller than the single-seater and after much fiddling around on the cockpit floor Hartley fired the beast up. It was the first time I had sat in a Lightning with both engines rumbling away somewhere aft. She felt like a ship. The lid came down and we taxied off at a reasonable Mach number to the threshold of Cranfield's runway, with the number two engine in fast idle (63% keeps the AC/DC online and results in fast taxi speeds). Lining up, Hartley took power and released the brakes, advanced to full power without reheat (these were

not serviceable yet) and we shot off down the runway. In what seemed like a second it was all over, throttles were shifted to idle/idle, the chute was pulled, clangers were going off, and before I knew it we were slowing down. A good and exhilarating test. Thank you, sir, I will take it!

With business being concluded we set about making plans to get XS452 serviceable. The original plan was to fly the aircraft to South Africa and to this end I bought two BAe Buccaneers, with one configured as a tanker to be the fuel donor on the way down. Any sensible chap would have done the same. The non-tanker Buccaneer, XW988 (now ZU-AVI), was successfully tested and flown out of the UK, arriving in Cape Town in April 1996 after a faultless flight.

Work was now well advanced on XS452. The SA CAA inspectors and I arrived in the UK to certify the aircraft for test flight purposes and to visit the British CAA in order to obtain test flight permission.

T5, XS451, was literally rebuilt from scratch over more than five years. The results speak for themselves.

'Live Red Top' Bob Bees, the squadron weapons officer, sits high on my wing as we transit to RAF Valley to fire a live missile.

After a very detailed inspection by the SA CAA, Chris Purnell (Principal Aeronautical Engineer) and Bill Rheede, the aircraft was approved for test flight and a test flight permit issued, subject to the British CAA giving permission for such flights. Much joy was proclaimed and even a few tears shed by some of the great British engineers who had strived for so long to get a Lightning back in the air.

On arrival in Gatwick House we met with officials of the British CAA who stated that under no circumstances were they going to allow the aircraft to fly in UK airspace, even on a South African permit, and even with the South African authority taking responsibility for the aircraft. Somewhat disillusioned and downcast we returned to South Africa to lick the wounds, both mental and financial, and to decide what to do next.

Well if it wasn't going to fly, having a Buccaneer tanker in the UK was pretty useless so we arranged for this aircraft to be ferried out. XW987 (now ZU-

BCR) arrived in South Africa, again after a near faultless flight, with the trusted crew of Keith Hartley and Peter Huett having completed two trans-Africa safaris – something of a world record I think.

Negotiations continued to obtain permission for the aircraft to fly in the UK. In the meantime I had ordered work on the aircraft to be stopped until we knew what was happening. After yet another trip and another fruitless representation to the British CAA I finally decided that this was the end and I should stop throwing good money after bad. I drove up to Cranfield for one last look at the aircraft and sat staring at it in the hangar. It had flat tyres now and was covered in dust – a really forlorn sight. I walked up to it and wrote 'Michael's Folly' in the dust.

Sitting there in the hangar was a defining moment and I remember being overcome with a resolve that I would not let the little grey people in officialdom beat me. Surely, what we are trying to do is a noble thing? Why can we get no help? Why do we get stonewalled at every turn?

I had learned the expressions of 'jobsworths' (not worth me job mate) and others less printable. But vision and courage will overcome – now I knew what Barry and his team had been up against for the better part of eight years. So, armed with this resolve I returned to South Africa and said to my lads, 'Lets go fetch' – another three words that would set off a chain of events and that could be a book in itself.

In the late spring of 1997 three South Africans arrived at Cranfield armed with toolboxes and a fair bit of fear at the daunting task confronting them. No Lightning had ever been dismantled and rebuilt as a flyer, but then again life is full of little challenges. More British team members were recruited, with Graeme Tagg and Ed Ford ably assisting the project. By now, the Cranfield authorities had also booted the aircraft out of the hangar as they needed the space. No other hangarage was available on the airfield so in South African parlance 'Die Boer maak a plan' which roughly translated means 'the farmer makes a plan'.

To this end, four 40ft containers were ordered and a makeshift hangar constructed into which XS452 was wheeled to commence the dismantling process. An office was set up inside one of the containers and each and every item disassembled was logged in a book and noted for reassembly. Each and every wire was tagged to ensure they all ended up being reconnected correctly – there could be nothing worse than switching on the battery master only for the main wheels to retract!

In retrospect, by not allowing the aircraft to fly the British CAA did us a favour in a number of ways. The aircraft was fundamentally sound but having broken it down we found a number of faults that, although not dangerous, would have caused problems in the future. Also, during rebuild we would be able to embody modifications and apply due care and attention to the wing center-section, notorious for fuel leaks.

It took the better part of three months to get XS452 into a condition that was suitable for shipping back to South Africa. Freezing weather and difficult technical conditions made the dismantling effort a job from hell, but finally in the autumn of

No other aircraft, apart from the F-104 Starfighter, can put a man in such a Dan Dare-like flying machine. This angle emphasises just how awesome a machine the Lightning is. The pilot sits astride two giant rockets – the ultimate buzz. XP693 is the last of Thunder City's Lightning fleet due for rebuild.

1997 the four containers left Cranfield bound for Cape Town, happily waved off by the South African team leader, (the late) Terry Cook, Boy Louw and Graeme Morcom.

Having sent off '452, I concluded a deal with Mach 2 Enterprises, a three-man consortium made up of Ernie Marshall, Brian Richardson and Barry Pover, who owned the two F6s and the T5, XS451. They too had realised that it was a fruitless exercise in attempting to get the Lightning to fly again in UK airspace. This purchase also included a vast amount of spares held at Kelly Brae in Cornwall.

So, hot on the heels of '452's departure more technicians arrived from South Africa and along with some willing local labour to get the spares shipped, '693, '773 and '451 were broken down and put into containers in a similar manner.

In the Southern Hemisphere spring of 1997, over a period of three weeks the general aviation area at Cape Town International Airport began to look like a container terminal. All in all, forty-eight 40ft

containers had arrived and the task of preparing the first Lightning for rebuild commenced. To assist us in our task, we had now built a 2,800sq m facility at Capetown airport, which we called AMARC (Aircraft Maintenance and Refurbishment Center).

To my knowledge no Lightnings had ever been split during squadron service and the wing reassembly jigs were not available. These we had to design from scratch. We made up a port and starboard trestle with adjustable pads so we could rig the wing for the join in all three axes. This kit would stand us in excellent stead for the rebuilds thereafter. So, on a bright spring day in the beautiful city of Cape Town, '452 was lifted on to her stands, front fuselage, rear fuselage and the two new wing trestles, and the rebuild got underway with great fervour.

Much planning and documentation had gone into the rebuild. Everything was listed and spares were drawn from the inventory but to find them was another story, so it was very much a 'search in that

Lightning sunset.

The way is was: viewed from
the right hand seat of T5,
XS452, Marc Ims holds station
on the other squadron T5,
XV328.

pile over there' kind of thing. At this stage I realised that it was probably best to let the experts get on with it and so I went off to fly.

The Buccaneers had arrived in Cape Town some time earlier and I thought I had better learn to fly one as the possibility of flying a Lightning at this stage was looking pretty remote. So once again the ever willing and able Keith Hartley arrived to do my Buccaneer training. After some intensive ground schooling this poor fellow had to sit in the back and speak to me in a high-pitched voice as off we went. There was no twin stick. I went solo four flights later and the feeling of deep respect for the machine and 'it's an honour, sir' is one that few will have in their lifetime. I can truly say the decision to fly the Buccaneer was one of my better ones.

Having got to understand the inner workings of the machine, I view it as one of the most remarkable pieces of engineering and conceptual ingenuity ever.

It is sad that this unsung hero of British genius never captured the hearts and souls of the public as much as some other types did.

Meanwhile, our trusted friends from Britain, Graham Tagg and Ed Ford, along with engine dude Geoff Commins, had arrived in South Africa to assist with the rebuild. What a great team we had assembled – to see these guys consumed with passion for the task and to witness the aircraft taking shape on a daily basis, I began to believe we might just do it.

And then on a bright summers day in February 1998 the T5, XS452, now resplendent in an all-black paint scheme, was wheeled out for its engine runs. Black had become a bit of a house 'colour' for Thunder City (as we had now named the company), sparked by the ex-Black Arrows Hunter F6 that we had acquired at the initial auction.

'Wheeee pfffffffft' as the Avpin starter spooled the

number one engine to life, and then a few minutes later another 'wheeee pffffffft' as the number two fired up. Crowds had come to see the spectacle and there was much excitement in the air. Everything was working pretty much as advertised. A lot of smoke came from the number one jet pipe, which was caused by grease and dirt burning off, but it soon went away. However, we could not get the AC/DC on line and it appeared that the Air Turbine Gear Box (ATGB) was dick and had to be replaced. More work, late nights, and skinned knuckles before Keith arrived for the reheat runs and test flights.

The SA CAA had also arrived to do the inspections and to issue the test flight permits. It was agreed that the first flight would be to the Test Flight and Development Center (TFDC) near the southern tip of Africa, avoiding built-up areas. We were to complete a satisfactory test flight programme at the base and then the CAA would be happy for the aircraft to return to Cape Town. The various bits of paper were concluded and issued. It was a great and refreshing change to work with the SA CAA who, while being naturally very cautious, were coming up with positive suggestions as to how all parties' requirements could be met. Colonel Des Barker, Officer Commanding of TFDC, was most accommodating in allowing the test programme to take place at a secret

On a bright summer's day in February 1998, T5, XS452, was wheeled out for her engine runs.

installation. It's great people like these who make you feel you are not alone.

More reheat runs. A problem was recurring on number two engine – we were getting a 'fuel two' warning caption but with much tweaking managed to get the caption to go out. Now we were all set.

At 1105hrs on 18 March 1998, XS452 took to the air with Keith Hartley in the left-hand seat and me in the right. The flight was dedicated to one of our British engineers, the late Baz Livesey, who had been such a stalwart throughout the program. Sadly he did not live to see '452 fly, having died of cancer some three months earlier.

The aircraft was relatively faultless and we turned out left, due south, for the base. It was just short of ten years since air was last under the wings of the great machine and being on that flight was so special that all thoughts of the clawing, fighting and scratching to get here were far from my mind.

My great friend Ralphie Garlick in his BAC Strikemaster flew the chase and had a somewhat intense American photographer on board who never released the negatives to us – he thought he was more important than the occasion.

We positioned for some air-to-air photography and then on to the base. The VHF was giving trouble through overheating and we switched it off for a minute and then back on – the comms came back but would deteriorate again with time. After fifteen minutes or so I asked the transfixed Hartley if I could take the stick.

'What? Oh, of course! Sorry!' he replied, brought back suddenly from his flight of nostalgia. Can't say I blame him. With my first grab of the stick we were tooling along at 300kts IAS at about 1,500ft – and I had the world's only flying Lightning in my hands! I was struck by how docile yet responsive she was, truly a delight to fly, but I had so much more to learn. And I was still to find out just how much of a delight she would truly become.

Back to Keith and we came barrelling down runway 17 at TFDC at 400kts for the initial and break to downwind. The whole base had come out to watch. A good flat approach at about 165kts IAS, over the fence and a firm arrival.

Keith grunted 'Rusty', idle/fast idle, chute. Call 'good chute'. Idle/idle, clangers go off as the ATGB goes offline. Kill the number one engine to reduce any residual thrust and turn off, dropping the chute near the retrieval vehicle.

We were marshalled in and shut down, and the seats made safe. Keith and I shook hands and climbed out to meet Des and the receiving officers of TFDC. It was the end of a very long and difficult road and the start of another one.

There were many confused emotions – satisfaction on one hand, a bit of ego and two fingers up to all those who said it couldn't be done and a bit of trepidation at the long road ahead – we still had another three to rebuild. Well, when one feels that way the best thing to do is go and have a big party. A whole convoy of people and equipment had now departed Cape Town. We had called them on arrival at TFDC and told them to leave for the base. They had been waiting at AMARC in case we turned back for technical or other reasons. This bunch arrived later and we all checked in to the mess and then on to a dinky little restaurant in Arniston, a small seaside village nearby. Great sports and much happiness and apparently I enjoyed myself very much.

With the dawn of day two a sprightly Hartley was all dressed and prepared for the first test flight sortie. Sitting alongside Keith and a little less sprightly, we prepared for the test flight going through the cards and the profile. Lining up on runway 08 Keith advanced to brake check power when the 'fuel two' caption lit up again – the gremlin was back. Back to the ramp and the lads clambered all over the aircraft to try and sort out the problem, but to no avail. This went on well into the night. It was quite a sight to see the Avon doing engine runs at full dry power at night, emitting a deep orange glow. We called the shut down at about 2300hrs. Clearly this was going to be an engine out job.

The team decision was to return to Cape Town and we flew back the following day, achieving only 93% power on the number two engine with the number one behaving perfectly. We were safe in the

Keith Hartley warned Mike that there are three dangerous things in a Lightning: fuel, fuel and fuel. Air-to-air refuelling went hand-in-hand with Lightning operations. Permanently short of fuel, VC10s, Victors and Vulcans were the Lightnings' lifelines.

knowledge that the Lightning has so much excess thrust that we could get airborne on one engine in dry power in just over 3,000ft of runway.

Eventually the problem was traced to the fuel/hydraulic heat exchanger, which is situated downstream of the filters – and it was so clogged that one could not see through it.

Slowly the beast settled down and became comfortable with flying again and the test flights were completed to Keith's satisfaction. She tried her best to throw out curved balls but the lads were always there to pick them up and sort them out. The SA CAA had now certified the aircraft and issued the relevant Certificate of Airworthiness. Again an

historic moment and the prized piece of paper was passed from team member to team member to see it for real.

And so to my training. With most aircraft one's respect for it grows as you get to know it better, while at the same time the aircraft becomes less intimidating and somehow seems to get smaller. Ground school (again) with Keith doing the talking (he really likes that). There are three dangerous things in a Lightning, he said: 'Fuel, fuel, fuel'. The rest was pretty straightforward and being fascinated by the workings of the machine I had swiped a Vol 1 (Master Maintenance Manual) for light bedtime reading. A word of advice: if you ever suffer from

Lightning flashback. One of my favourite Lightning pictures: a pair of 11 Squadron F6s return to Akrotiri after a gun firing sortie.

insomnia: read the Vol 1 – you will be gone in an instant.

Keith did the first couple of sorties with me in the left-hand seat and I really starting to get to love the handling qualities of the aircraft. Sadly, Keith had to return to BAe for something ridiculous like work and he swapped places with Craig Penrice, a former Lightning pilot and ETPS test pilot, now with BAe Systems. Craig completed my training and was happy (I think) to send me solo.

Full of butterflies I fired her up – I was very conscious of the empty right-hand seat – and taxied out to the threshold of runway 19. It seemed that the whole airport had come to a standstill. More pressure. Lining up, I advanced the power gingerly to about 85% holding on the brakes, being very careful to bring the slower number one engine up to symmetric RPM (number one idles at 35%, two at 63% for the ATGB AC/DC) so as not to over-temp the number one. Releasing the brakes while

simultaneously advancing to full dry power, '452 hurtled off and at 135kts IAS I pulled back on the stick to get the nose flying and she unstuck at about 170kts. Brakes on and gear up and I was solo (no flap for take-off on the T5).

Craig had signed me out solo in the circuit and I did only one retraction and selected gear down on the downwind leg. I then left the gear down for the remaining four low over-shoots as each gear cycle is fatigued. During the solo '452 threw a few captions at me – I had a 'pump s', the VHF went 'wonky', the airbrake gauge failed indicating 'out' (but with so much thrust who cares anyway!), and a few others just to let me know who was the boss.

I can claim a good landing because the right-hand seat was empty and the tyres remained intact, the chute worked well and I taxied back to the ramp. Shutting down there was a whole lot of smiling and expectant faces looking up at me. Craig removed the ladder as is customary and eventually I got back on

Waiting to go.

the ground with much congratulations all round. However, business first, and I called over Terry Cook, (our late Chief Engineer who was so thin he was affectionately known as our skeleton crew) and gave him a bollocking for the wobblies on the aircraft. I suppose the tension had got to me and before I dampened the whole occasion Craig wisely tapped me on the shoulder and said 'Lighten up mate – you've just gone solo in a Lightning!' He was right of course, so off to the pub and a great evening was had by all.

Some of the greatest learning you do by yourself and my next twenty or so sorties were really about 'getting to know you' as the song goes. I cannot claim to know the aircraft well yet, but a definite bond has developed and with every flight one learns more about the incredible collective genius behind the aircraft and the true character she demonstrates. Keith and Craig deserve a vote of thanks for having the courage, skills and patience to teach a relatively

inexperienced pilot like me to fly one of the all-time great aircraft.

'452 has now logged over 100 sorties and she has settled down into being a wonderful and reliable jet. Needless to say she is loved and nurtured at every turn but the early days gave her the nickname 'Big Bad Dog' – her registration BBD. As our 'first-born' we will always have a particularly soft spot for her.

While all this was going on we had commenced the spares draw for the rebuild of XS451. This was going to be a far bigger and more daunting task because the aircraft was largely incomplete. '451 had very low fatigue and her airframe was in superb condition. Once again the trusted British team of Graeme Tagg, Ed Ford and Geoff Commins were having to slum it in the African sun, beavering away and providing training on type for the additional local ex-SAAF engineers we had employed.

Thanks to the huge inventory we were able to

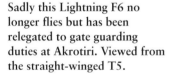

Sadly this Lightning F6 no longer flies but has been relegated to gate guarding duties at Akrotiri. Viewed from the straight-winged T5.

install new components throughout – virtually 90%, and she really was taking shape extremely well. We had elected to get rid of the old UHF system and install new VHF dual comms in both '451 and '452 with new supersonic rated aerials. The cockpit of '451 was virtually rebuilt from the floor upwards and when finished it was like new. It was a great tribute to our resident chief 'sparktrician', Peter Cole, who rewired the entire cockpit and got it all working so well.

The experience gained on '452 proved invaluable on '451 and I doubt if this rebuild could have been completed as successfully without the school fees we had paid for so dearly on '452. From the start of the spares draw to the first engine runs it took fourteen months of hard labour, but the results were worth it. Having been in storage and under cover, the skin on '451 was in good condition. The aircraft had never been painted and a fair bit of good-natured pressure was put on me to keep the aircraft in its original silver livery to which I agreed, subject to a paint job if the skin deteriorated in any way.

It was another lovely summer's day when the gleaming silver beast was rolled out to see daylight again as a complete aircraft, the first time since being placed into storage in 1977. The rebuild team fired her up with both starters performing perfectly. Once again the customary smoke emissions indicated that dirt and grease were burning off inside the jet pipes. There were lots of problems with the motion boxes on the throttles, but eventually we got this to the correct idle and fast idle settings.

As with most rebuilds you can virtually hear the aircraft saying 'I think these people are serious – they are actually going to fly me!' And then they start to throw out major resistance. '451 was no different in this respect and snags too numerous to mention began appearing. No sooner was one solved than the next appeared.

Backlit against the southern sun, XR773 formates on the camera ship during a photo sortie in August 2002.

Our faithful test pilot Hartley had arrived again and was busy problem solving with the engineering crews. Keith is different to most in that he has an extensive technical knowledge (and doesn't fly that badly either!) of the aircraft and is able to communicate the snags in great detail, which assists the engineers tremendously. However, time was running out as I was due to go to England on business and sadly had to leave the lads beavering away.

Three days later I was at the Goodwood Festival of Speed when my mobile phone rang. It was Barry. 'She's airborne!' he proclaimed triumphantly.

'Well done!' I replied. 'Please congratulate the lads for me – and call me when he is down.'

Being a Lightning T5 I did not have too long to wait before the mobile rang again and it was Keith. He ran over the sortie that had been largely faultless other than some auto-stab problems and a slightly hot number two. But his tone was infectious and clearly he was most excited and pleased with the aircraft.

The test program was completed and the SA CAA arrived to do the inspections and release the Certificate of Airworthiness. It was interesting to note the great pride shown by the SA CAA in being associated with the project.

Anyone who has had the privilege of getting up close to ZU-BEX/XS451 (now affectionately known as Sexy Bexy) will see the quality of workmanship that both our British and South African engineers have put into the project. The aircraft is in polished silver and if one looks into the cockpit or wheel bays it is easy to see the aircraft is like new and in showroom condition.

I remember my first flight in BEX very well because I received a classic after-departure clearance from the ever willing and helpful Cape Town ATC. I was lined up on the southerly runway 19 due to fly north to the military training area and it went something like this:

'Bravo Echo X-ray, after departure teardrop back

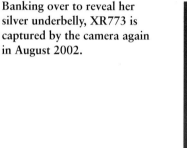

Banking over to reveal her silver underbelly, XR773 is captured by the camera again in August 2002.

onto zero one, commence climb abeam the tower, no speed or altitude restrictions.'

Bless him – I will comply, Sir!

Getting airborne in dry power I turned back. Coming over the fence at about 250kts IAS and 100ft heading north I lit both burners and, as duly instructed, rotated abeam the tower (now doing about 500kts) and disappeared vertically into the African sky as only this incredible machine can. The power of the aircraft is something to marvel at. In the vertical one can see the indicated airspeed decaying as the air rapidly gets thinner and the Mach meter starts coming up – and I capped off at 20 000ft inverted and pulling three G. Eat your heart out F-15!

I returned some 30 minutes later after a faultless flight (other than the auto-stab playing up a bit again) and did a beat-up of the tower and a break to land. Sadly, the old fun detector got a lock on us and those days of coming past the tower low and fast have been reduced to zone speed of 210kts – only reasonable I suppose.

It is a tribute to the build and engineering standards that both aircraft, BBD and BEX, behave identically apart from the trim settings on BEX being slightly offset to counteract drag from the refuelling probe.

By the time '451 took to the air for the first time, the single-seat Lightning F6, XR773, was on her

For unknown reasons, XR773 was always kept in a more pristine condition than other Lightnings. It also had a relatively low fatigue life, having been involved in an accident earlier in its career that kept the aircraft on the ground for many months. As of November 2002 she is the only single-seat Lightning flying anywhere in the world.

Thunder City's massive complex has its own taxiway onto Cape Town International Airport.

stands and ready for assembly. As with the previous two aircraft, much attention was given to the spares draw and planning the rebuild. With two successful projects now under our belt things naturally went more smoothly this time. Both engine bays were stripped and completely rebuilt, new engines and reheat pipes installed, new communications equipment fitted along with an altitude encoder. (Lightnings never had mode Charlie and this is now connected to the weapons pack altimeter.)

'773 (now BEW, but as yet no nickname, although it might have something to do with whiskey) took to the air on 4 November 2001, some thirteen years after the Lightning went out of RAF service. I had the privilege of being the testing pilot on this occasion. Taking the power on the brakes, holding RPM, everything was normal and I released the brakes and advanced to full dry power. I was performing a dry power take-off with flaps down and at about 100kts the Strip Speed Indicator failed.

Having checked the standby ASI, I elected to continue the sortie, lifting off at about 175kts IAS, gear and flap up, and continued due south to the designated air test area.

Setting both nozzles to 'cruise', or about 88% power, the beast was still climbing like the proverbial homesick angel. Amazingly, after having last flown in 1992 on a delivery flight from BAe's Warton facility to Exeter, then subjected to a complete dismantling, shipped halfway around the world and rebuilt, all she needed was a twitch of aileron trim and a tad of down elevator and the aircraft flew hands off into the ether. At which point I started to laugh – what an absolute honour to be flying the only operational Lightning F6 in existence on a perfect day in an aircraft that felt and behaved like she had just come off the shop floor. Sometimes you inherently know that a machine is good and BEW was just that. I felt an overriding sense of security and solidarity with the machine – assisted

by the fact one has an extra 2,000lb of fuel on board!

Having successfully completed the first portion of the air-test schedule I returned to Cape Town International Airport for two low overshoots. Interestingly, as one gets to know the aircraft better your awareness of what should or should not be increases. Indicating about 200kts on the standby ASI (which is the size of a bottle top) the alpha of the aircraft felt wrong, too flat, which intimates that the standby ASI was under reading and I was fast. In order to calibrate this I accelerated the aircraft to see at what speed the flaps automatically retracted (the aircraft is fitted with a flap over speed device) and these went away at about 215kts IAS, about 35kts too fast – work out the inertia of one half mv squared at 35kts and it makes quite a significant difference!

Anyway, the impromptu calibration worked and I touched down at an indicated 125kts – 160 actual after a near perfect test flight, the only problems

being the ASI (both), minor auto-stab corrections needed and the SWP (Standard Warning Panel) cover falling off which I placed in my suit pocket. Not too bad I would say! With these matters attended to, the second flight was conducted in the TFDC airspace at FL400 where Mach 1.8 was achieved and the balance of the upper air-work test schedule completed.

The aircraft was awarded her Certificate of Airworthiness and has been performing magnificently. She has retained her markings for now and made her display debut at the Stellenbosch Airshow in the Western Cape, on 15 December 2001, setting off car alarms and causing a noise mayhem that thousands had come to experience.

The Lightning fleet as of November 2002 comprised two T5s – XS451 and XS452, and F6, XR773. At that stage XP693 was in the process of being surveyed and planned for the final rebuild. '693 had never been taken into RAF service, instead having been operated by BAe for many years. It was the

XR773 (now BEW, but as yet no nickname) took to the air again on 4 November 2001, thirteen years after the Lightning went out of RAF service.

Tornado development chase plane and was flown many times in this role by none other than Keith Hartley. A vast amount of resource and effort has already gone into making the support infrastructure for the rebuild of '693 complete, and it is hoped that this aircraft will take to the skies again and be as wonderful and successful as the previous three.

My relationship with the Lightning and the project as a whole thus far has got to be the most challenging and rewarding time any man could hope for in one lifetime. The mountains climbed, the paradigms shifted, the highs and lows experienced and the friendships made have it all in one basket. Today, the future has never looked brighter for the preservation of a handful of these examples of the greatest interceptor fighter of all time, albeit in a land only an overnight flight away.

I still find the Lightning a supremely inspiring aircraft. Whenever I walk up to one I have a quiet feeling of pride that we, as a family of people with a common goal, have breathed life into dead pieces of aluminium and steel and they now are preserved for posterity in the place where they belong – the sky.

The Thunder City Flying Company is the only military jet outfit in the world to be accredited with a SA CAA Part 141 License. Today it runs a fleet of eighteen aircraft comprising mainly of Lightnings, Buccaneers and Hunters. The company is a registered training institution and has a joint venture with the National Test Pilot School of Mojave, California, USA, the largest test pilot training facility in the world. It also has a joint venture with a number of postgraduate learning institutions to market Executive Flight Path, an executive and leadership training programme designed to instill discipline and processes in today's business leaders through the medium of military jet operations. The company also encourages flights in the jets by well-heeled individuals who wish to have the ultimate thrill.

Based at Thunder City's massive 14,000sq m complex with its own taxiway onto Cape Town International Airport, the fleet is also accessible to the public and guided tours are offered on most days. The aircraft can be seen at air shows throughout South Africa and have been featured in a number of television commercials and programs.

It was seen as important by both Thunder City and the SA CAA that a reasonable and safe method of commercial operation be achieved in order to preserve the machines, operate to the highest standards and gain sufficient revenues to maintain these standards. It is indeed a tribute to the farsightedness and creative thinking of the SA CAA that the company was awarded its status. Through its very high level of engineering and operational staff it has achieved an impeccable operating record. A massive spares inventory ensures that the aircraft will run for many years to come.

Binbrook Lightning Fates

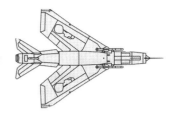

The following is a list of the Lightnings kept at RAF Binbrook as of February 1986 and their eventual fates after the type was withdrawn from service.

Lightning F.3

XP694 First flight 1/5/63, last flight August 1984. Scrapped April 1988 and sent to Otterburn range to act as target

XP695 First flight 20/6/63, last flight 15/3/84. Acted as airfield decoy, then scrapped September 1987

XP701 First flight 14/9/63, scrapped late 1987. Nose section preserved at Hawkinge museum

XP702 First flight 19/9/63, last flight 28/8/82. Placed in storage, but never flew again. Scrapped April 1988, remains sent to Otterburn ranges

XP706 First flight 28/10/63, last flight July 1985. Preserved by the Bomber County Museum at Hemswell, Lincs.

XP707 First flight 13/11/63, last flight 19/3/87. Crashed whilst performing aerobatics over Binbrook airfield

XP741 First flight 4/2/64, last flight September 1987. Delivered to RAF Manston for fire training

XP748 First flight 4/5/64, last flight February 1975, then stored for two years before being used as a gate guardian until the summer of 1988. Removed from gate and scrapped, remains sent to Pendine range

XP749 First flight 11/12/63, last flight October 1986. Scrapped December 1987

XP750 First flight 3/1/64, last flight November 1984. Scrapped December 1987

XP751 First flight 16/3/64, last flight October 1986. Aircraft damaged beyond repair with rear fuselage fire. Scrapped December 1987

XP761 First flight 3/11/64, last flight 14/10/74, then used as a ground instructional airframe until scrapped in January 1988

XP764 First flight 19/9/64, last flight October 1986. Scrapped January 1988

XR713 First flight 21/10/64, last flight 11/3/87. Delivered to RAF Leuchars and kept by No. 111 Sqn.

XR716 First flight 19/11/64, last flight September 1987. Delivered to RAF Cottesmore as fire training aircraft and burnt

XR718 First flight 14/12/64, last flight 2/2/87. Delivered to RAF Wattisham as battle damage repair aircraft, then given to the Blyth Valley Aviation Society of Suffolk on 19 May 1993

XR720 First flight 24/12/64, last flight 6/2/85. Scrapped January 1988

XR749 First flight 30/4/65, last flight February 1987. Delivered to RAF Leuchars as battle damage repair airframe. Preserved at Teeside Airport in 1995

XR751 First flight 31/5/65, final flight September 1982. Preserved in Cornwall

Lightning T.5

XS416 First flight 20/8/64, last flight 21/12/87. Preserved at NATO Aircraft Museum, Grainthorpe, Lincs

XS417 First flight 17/7/64, last flight 18/5/87. Preserved at the Newark Air Museum

XS418 First flight 18/12/64, last flight September 1974. Used as surface decoy until scrapped in September 1987

XS419 First flight 18/12/64, last flight 27 February 1987. Scrapped July 1993

XS420 First flight 23/1/65, last flight May 1983. Preserved at Walpole St Andrews, Norfolk

XS423 First flight 31/5/65, last flight 1974, then used as airfield decoy until scrapped in September 1987

XS449 First flight 30/4/65, last flight September 1974. Used as decoy then scrapped September 1987

XS450 First flight 25/5/65, last flight January 1975. Scrapped September 1987

XS452 First flight 30/6/65, last flight 30/6/88. Delivered to Cranfield and preserved

XS454 First flight 6/7/65, last flight June 1975. Used as decoy until September 1987 then scrapped

XS456 First flight 26/10/65, last flight January 1987. Preserved Wainfleet

XS457 First flight 8/11/65, last flight 9/12/83. Damaged on landing and stored until late 1987 then scrapped. Nose section preserved near Grimsby

XS458 First flight 3/12/65, last flight 30/6/88. Delivered to Cranfield

XS459 First flight 18/12/65, last flight 15/3/87. Preserved Fenland Aviation Museum

XV328 First flight 22/12/66, last flight 30/6/88. Stored at Phoenix Aviation, Bruntingthorpe

Lightning F.6

XR724 First flight 10/2/65, last flight 29/7/92. Preserved at Binbrook

XR725 First flight 19/2/65, last flight 17/12/87. Preserved at Binbrook

XR726 First flight 26/2/65, last flight 24/8/87. Scrapped, nose preserved at Harrogate

XR727 First flight 8/3/65, last flight 10/5/88. Flown to RAF Wildenrath to act as battle damage repair airframe then scrapped

XR728 First flight 17/3/65, last flight 24/6/88. Preserved at Bruntingthorpe

XR747 First flight 2/4/65, last flight 14/8/87. Scrapped, nose preserved by the Lightning Flying Club

XR752 First flight 16/6/65, last flight 8/1/86. Grounded after in-flight fire then scrapped in September 1987

XR753 First flight 23/6/65, last flight 24/5/88. Delivered to RAF Leeming as battle damage repair airframe but preserved by No. 11 Sqn

XR754   First flight 8/7/65, last flight 24/6/88. delivered to RAF Honington as battle damage repair airframe and scrapped in 1992, nose section preserved

XR755   First flight 15/7/65, last flight December 1987. Preserved by Castle Air of Cornwall

XR756   First flight 11/8/65, last flight December 1987. Preserved by Mr E. Marshall of Cornwall

XR757   First flight 19/8/65, last flight December 1987. Scrapped, nose section preserved

XR758   First flight 30/8/65, last flight 12/5/88. Delivered to RAF Laarbruch as battle damage repair airframe

XR759   First flight 9/9/65, last flight 29/9/87. Scrapped nose section preserved

XR763   First flight 15/10/65, last flight 1/7/87. Crashed RAF Akrotiri, Cyprus

XR769   First flight 1/12/65, last flight 11/4/88. Crashed North Sea

XR770   First flight 16/12/65, last flight April 1988. Preserved in Grimsby

XR771   First flight 20/1/66, last flight 15/3/88. Preserved at the Midland Counties Museum, Coventry

XR773   First flight 28/2/66, last flight 23/12/92. Preserved at Thunder City, Cape Town, S. Africa

XS895   First flight 6/4/66, last flight December 1987. Scrapped, delivered to Pendine range as target

XS897   First flight 10/5/66, last flight 14/12/87. Preserved at the South Yorkshire Air Museum, Firbeck

XS898   First flight 20/5/66, last flight 30/6/88. Preserved by Tony Collins, Lavendon, Bucks

XS899   First flight 8/6/66, last flight 30/6/88. Preserved by Charles Ross, RAF Coltishall

XS901   First flight 1/7/66, last flight 12/5/88. Delivered to RAF Brüggen as battle damage repair airframe

XS903   First flight 17/8/66, last flight 10/5/88. Delivered to the Yorkshire Air Museum, Elvington

XS904   First flight 26/8/66, last flight January 1993. Last Lightning to fly, delivered to Bruntingthorpe and preserved

XS919   First flight 28/9/66, last flight 15/3/88. Preserved at Devonport

XS922   First flight 6/12/66, last flight 14/6/88. Delivered to RAF Wattisham as battle damage aircraft, cockpit preserved

XS923   First flight 13/12/66, last flight 30/6/88. Preserved at Welshpool, Powys

XS925   First flight 28/2/67, last flight September 1987. Preserved at RAF Museum Hendon

XS927   First flight 15/2/67, last flight October 1986. Scrapped by March 1988

XS928   First flight 28/2/67, last flight August 1992. Preserved at Warton

XS929   First flight 1/3/67, last flight 20/5/88. Delivered to RAF Akrotiri as gate-guard

XS932   First flight 9/4/67, last flight October 1986. Scrapped, nose section preserved

XS933   First flight 27/4/67, last flight October 1986. Scrapped by April 1988, nose section preserved

XS935   First flight 29/5/67, last flight September 1987. Scrapped

XS936   First flight 31/5/67, last flight October 1987. Preserved Liskeard, Cornwall

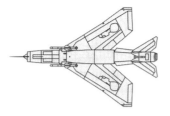

APPENDIX 2

Squadron Badges

5 Squadron official badge.

11 Squadron official badge.

Lightning aircrew patch.

Lightning aircrew patch.

11 Squadron flying suit badge.

The coveted Single Seat Air Defence badge.

The 1,000 Hours patch awarded to pilots who had flown in excess of 1,000 hours on type.

You can almost smell the burning rubber as XS903 'BA' touches down at a little over 170mph. It's easy to see how, on a strong cross wind, a Lightning's tyres could be worn out during a single take off and landing. This particular airframe is preserved intact at the Yorkshire Air Museum at Elvington. Appropriately its last flight was performed by Wg Cdr Jake Jarron, whose name appeared under the cockpit.